CLARK C. WILLIAMS

33rd Degree Knowledge
Mastering Consciousness, Vibrations and Energy Fields

Copyright © 2024 by Clark C. Williams

All rights reserved. No part of this publication may be reproduced, stored or transmitted in any form or by any means, electronic, mechanical, photocopying, recording, scanning, or otherwise without written permission from the publisher. It is illegal to copy this book, post it to a website, or distribute it by any other means without permission.

First edition

This book was professionally typeset on Reedsy.
Find out more at reedsy.com

Contents

1. The 33rd Degree: Unveiling the Secrets of an Enigmatic Realm — 1
2. Understanding Energy Frequencies: The Cosmic Symphony — 6
3. Identifying Your Personal Energy Signature: Self-Discovery — 12
4. Balancing Your Chakras: Harmonizing the Energy Centers — 18
5. Developing Intuition Through Meditation: Tapping into the... — 24
6. Decoding Energy Patterns: The Cosmic Symphony — 30
7. The Power of Resonance and Vibration: Harmonizing with the... — 34
8. Harmonizing with the Universal Field: Becoming a Conduit for... — 39
9. Sensing and Reading Energy Fields: Becoming a Master of... — 45
10. Shielding Yourself from Negative Energy: Protecting Your... — 50
11. Amplifying Intentions with Visualization: Manifesting Your... — 55
12. Tuning into the Energy of Others: Empathetic Perception — 60
13. Recognizing and Releasing Blockages: Clearing the Path to... — 65
14. Mastering the Art of Energetic Projection: Shaping Reality... — 71

15	Protecting Your Energy From Draining: Forging Your Energetic...	76
16	Navigating the Multidimensional Realms : Lattice Of...	80
17	The Role Of Breathwork In Energy Control : The Bridge Of...	85
18	Activating the Third Eye and Crown: A Journey Towards...	90
19	Deciphering Symbols and Energy Codes	95
20	Transmuting Negative Energy Patterns	100
21	Working with Elemental Energies	106
22	Developing a Personal Energy Practice	111
23	Integrating 33rd Degree Knowledge into Daily Life	116
24	A Symphony of Enlightenment	122

1

The 33rd Degree: Unveiling the Secrets of an Enigmatic Realm

"The universe is not only stranger than we imagine; it is stranger than we can imagine."

The human mind, a marvel of complexity, is capable of feats that defy explanation. It can conjure dreams, solve equations, and even compose symphonies. Yet, there remains a vast expanse of untapped potential within each of us, a realm of knowledge and power that lies dormant, waiting to be awakened. This realm, shrouded in mystery and intrigue, is known as the 33rd Degree.

The 33rd Degree is not a mere concept or belief; it is a profound state of consciousness, a level of understanding that transcends the limitations of the ordinary mind. It is a place where the veil between the seen and the unseen is lifted, where the laws of physics and metaphysics intertwine, and where the power of thought becomes a tangible force.

To embark on the journey to the 33rd Degree is to embark on a quest for self-discovery, for spiritual enlightenment, and for the mastery of one's own destiny. It is a path that demands courage, discipline, and an unwavering commitment to truth.

Along the way, you will encounter a labyrinth of symbols, rituals, and esoteric teachings that have been passed down through the ages. These ancient wisdoms hold the keys to unlocking the hidden potential within you, and they offer a roadmap to navigate the uncharted territories of the 33rd Degree.

In the quest for deeper understanding, we encounter the profound wisdom of the 33rd Degree—a pinnacle of spiritual evolution that invites seekers to embark on a journey of discovery. This degree offers insights into energetic realms and the hidden forces that shape our reality. Let us begin by contemplating the duality that pervades existence, characterized by the interplay of light and darkness. This concept of duality serves not only as a philosophical cornerstone but also as a practical guide in our lives.

The duality encapsulated in the symbol of the double-headed eagle is one of balance and unity. This majestic creature, revered across cultures, becomes a representation of how opposing forces can harmoniously co-exist. With its two heads looking in different directions, it embodies the essential idea that the spiritual and material realms are interconnected. The double-headed eagle, often associated with Freemasonry, signifies the need for understanding and embracing duality as a pathway to true enlightenment.

To illustrate this concept, consider the balance between knowledge and ignorance. Knowledge is often viewed as a source of light, illuminating the path ahead, while ignorance can be likened to darkness, obscuring our vision and limiting our potential. The journey toward enlightenment requires us to confront and reconcile these opposing forces within ourselves. By acknowledging our ignorance, we create space for growth and learning, allowing the light of knowledge to penetrate the shadows of our understanding.

The double-headed eagle also symbolizes the merging of different perspectives. One head gazes toward the past, drawing upon the wisdom and lessons it holds, while the other looks to the future, embracing change and innovation. This duality represents the spiritual journey of continuous learning, growth, and adaptation. In our lives, we often encounter situations that require us to balance tradition with progress. By integrating the insights gained from our experiences with the aspirations we hold for the future, we can navigate the complexities of existence with greater clarity and purpose.

Sacred geometry plays a vital role in underpinning these teachings, revealing the divine order and interconnectedness of all life. The Flower of Life, for instance, is a geometric figure composed of multiple overlapping circles, symbolizing the rhythm and patterns inherent in the universe. Each shape within the Flower of Life reflects unique vibrational frequencies, akin to musical notes in a grand symphony, reminding us of the harmonious structure that governs our existence.

To understand the significance of sacred geometry, consider how it manifests in nature. From the spirals of galaxies to the intricate patterns of a sunflower, these geometric forms are not merely aesthetic; they represent the underlying principles that govern the universe. The Fibonacci sequence, for example, is a mathematical pattern found in various natural phenomena, including the arrangement of leaves on a stem and the branching of trees. This sequence illustrates how nature adheres to specific ratios and proportions, creating a sense of harmony and balance.

By contemplating these geometric forms, we attune ourselves to the universal principles governing reality. Sacred geometry serves as a bridge between the material and spiritual realms, allowing us to access deeper levels of understanding. When we engage with these patterns, we open ourselves to the possibility of transformation, aligning our consciousness with the rhythms of the cosmos.

Furthermore, we must attune ourselves to the vibrational frequencies inherent in sacred texts and rituals. Throughout history, cultures have harnessed the power of sound and resonance as tools for transformation. Ancient chants and mantras, steeped in tradition, serve as vehicles for aligning one's consciousness with higher realms. The vibrations produced through these practices not only elevate individuals but also create a communal experience that fosters collective spiritual growth.

For example, consider the practice of chanting "Om," a sacred sound in Hinduism and Buddhism. This single syllable is believed to encompass the essence of the universe, representing the interconnectedness of all existence. When chanted, "Om" produces a vibrational frequency that resonates within the body, promoting a sense of peace and alignment with the cosmos. This practice exemplifies how sound can serve as a catalyst for spiritual awakening, allowing individuals to transcend the limitations of the material world.

The use of sound in spiritual practices is not limited to Eastern traditions. In various cultures, drumming, singing, and other forms of musical expression have been employed to create altered states of consciousness. These practices facilitate a deeper connection to the divine, allowing practitioners to access higher realms of awareness. By engaging with these vibrational frequencies, we can elevate our consciousness and align ourselves with the energies that govern our existence.

By integrating these teachings, one can unlock the mystical dimensions of reality. The pursuit of mastery over energy fields allows us not only to shape our personal destinies but also to influence the world around us positively. Each lesson in this chapter illuminates the path to enlightenment, urging us to delve deeper into the mysteries that lie at our feet.

The journey to the 33rd Degree is not for the faint of heart. It requires dedication, perseverance, and a willingness to confront your deepest fears and insecurities. But for those who are willing to make the commitment, the rewards are immeasurable.

By unlocking the secrets of the 33rd Degree, you can tap into a source of infinite power, wisdom, and love. You can heal yourself, transform your life, and make a positive impact on the world.

The 33rd Degree is a realm of infinite possibilities. It is a place where dreams become reality, where miracles happen, and where the human spirit soars to new heights.

2

Understanding Energy Frequencies: The Cosmic Symphony

"Everything is energy and that it is possible to control energy."

Imagine the universe as a grand symphony, a harmonious composition of countless vibrations. From the tiniest atom to the vast expanse of galaxies, everything is vibrating at a unique frequency. These vibrations, often imperceptible to our physical senses, are the fundamental building blocks of reality.

Energy frequencies are more than just abstract concepts; they are tangible forces that shape our experiences and influence our lives. They are the invisible threads that connect us to everything around us, from the smallest particle to the vast cosmos.

To understand the 33rd Degree, it is essential to grasp the nature of energy frequencies. They are the language of the universe, a dialect that can be learned and mastered. By understanding this language, we can

UNDERSTANDING ENERGY FREQUENCIES: THE COSMIC SYMPHONY

begin to unlock the hidden potential within ourselves and influence the world around us.

Imagine energy frequencies as a vast ocean, a sea of vibrations that permeate every aspect of our existence. Each thought, emotion, and action sends ripples through this ocean, influencing and being influenced by the greater cosmic current.

To truly understand the essence of energy frequency, one must first appreciate the fundamental vibrations that underpin the fabric of the universe. These vibrations resonate through every atom, every thought, and every emotion, forming the very basis of our existence. They are not mere abstract concepts; they are tangible forces that shape our reality in profound ways. Imagine these frequencies as the cosmic heartbeat—a pulse that dictates the rhythm of existence itself. Each frequency oscillates at various wavelengths, carrying its own unique signature and potential.

In this intricate dance of energy, we discover that frequencies are the very essence of life and consciousness. Picture them as the unseen threads weaving through the fabric of your being. Every emotion you feel, every thought you think, sends ripples through this energetic ocean, influencing and being influenced by the greater cosmic current. This interplay of vibrations is what mystics and sages have long referred to as the universal energy field.

To grasp this concept fully, we must explore its symbolic interpretations. Frequencies can be seen as the language of the cosmos—a dialect that we can tune into and manipulate with our minds. Visualize yourself as a conductor orchestrating the symphony of energies around you. By aligning with specific frequencies, you can harmonize your internal vibrations with those of the universe, achieving a state of synchronicity and heightened awareness.

This knowledge is not merely academic; it is experiential. You must feel these vibrations, attune your senses to their subtleties, and learn to differentiate between the myriad frequencies that permeate your existence. Through this attunement, you will begin to reveal the secrets of mental control over the energy field, laying the foundation for deeper exploration into the domains of 33rd Degree knowledge.

At the core of this understanding is the recognition that everything in the universe is energy, vibrating at different frequencies. This idea is not new; it has been echoed by thinkers throughout history. Nikola Tesla famously said, "If you want to find the secrets of the universe, think in terms of energy, frequency, and vibration." His insight points to a fundamental truth: the universe operates on a set of energetic principles that govern how we interact with the world around us.

To delve deeper into the nature of energy frequencies, we can look at how they manifest in our emotional lives. Every emotion we experience has a corresponding vibrational frequency. For instance, feelings of love, joy, and gratitude resonate at higher frequencies, while emotions such as fear, anger, and sadness vibrate at lower frequencies. This distinction is crucial because our emotional state directly influences our energetic output and, consequently, our experiences in life.

When we operate at a lower vibrational frequency, we often find ourselves trapped in cycles of negativity and stagnation. Chronic stress, negative self-talk, and toxic relationships can all contribute to this state. In contrast, when we elevate our vibrational frequency through positive thoughts and emotions, we unlock our potential for growth and fulfillment. High vibrational energy is characterized by feelings of optimism, resilience, and a sense of purpose.

Understanding the relationship between thoughts and energy is essential. Our thoughts are powerful tools that can either elevate or diminish our vibrational state. Positive thoughts, such as affirmations of self-worth and gratitude, can raise our frequency and align us with higher energies. Conversely, negative thoughts rooted in doubt and fear can lower our vibrational state, creating barriers to our personal growth.

To illustrate this concept, consider the practice of mindfulness. Engaging in mindfulness techniques—such as meditation, deep breathing, or simply being present in the moment—can help us cultivate a higher vibrational state. By focusing on the here and now, we can release negative thought patterns and emotional blockages, allowing the natural flow of energy to return to our lives.

Moreover, the concept of emotional energy extends beyond individual experiences; it has a ripple effect on our surroundings. Research has shown that our emotional states can influence not only our well-being but also the energy of those around us. When we radiate high vibrational energy, we create a positive environment that can uplift others. Conversely, low vibrational energy can create an atmosphere of tension and discomfort.

This interconnectedness is a fundamental aspect of the universal energy field. Just as each note in a symphony contributes to the overall harmony, each individual's energy influences the collective vibration of the community. By consciously raising our own vibrational frequency, we contribute to a more harmonious reality for ourselves and those around us.

To further explore the concept of energy frequencies, we can look at the principles of sacred geometry. Sacred geometry illustrates how patterns and shapes in nature resonate with specific frequencies. For example, the Flower of Life, composed of interconnected circles, represents the interconnectedness of all existence. Each shape within this pattern vibrates at its own frequency, contributing to the overall harmony of the design.

By contemplating these geometric forms, we can attune ourselves to the universal principles that govern reality. Sacred geometry serves as a bridge between the material and spiritual realms, allowing us to access deeper levels of understanding. When we engage with these patterns, we open ourselves to the possibility of transformation, aligning our consciousness with the rhythms of the cosmos.

In addition to sacred geometry, we can also explore the role of sound in influencing energy frequencies. Sound is a potent tool for transformation, as it carries vibrational frequencies that can affect our emotional and physical states. Music, chanting, and even the spoken word can elevate our vibrational frequency and promote healing.

For instance, consider the practice of sound healing, which utilizes specific frequencies to promote relaxation and emotional release. Instruments like singing bowls, gongs, and tuning forks produce vibrations that resonate with our energy fields, facilitating a state of harmony and balance. By immersing ourselves in these sounds, we can experience profound shifts in our emotional and energetic states.

The connection between sound and energy frequencies is further exemplified in the study of brain waves. Our brain operates at different frequencies depending on our state of consciousness. From the deep relaxation of delta waves to the heightened awareness of gamma waves, each frequency corresponds to a specific mental state. By understanding and manipulating these frequencies, we can enhance our cognitive abilities and emotional well-being.

Incorporating practices that elevate our vibrational frequency into our daily lives is essential for personal growth. This can include engaging in activities that bring us joy, surrounding ourselves with positive influences, and practicing gratitude. By consciously choosing to focus on the positive aspects of life, we can raise our energetic vibrations and align ourselves with higher frequencies.

Today, modern science is beginning to validate these ancient teachings. Scientists have discovered that everything in the universe, from atoms to galaxies, is composed of energy vibrating at different frequencies. This understanding has led to the development of new technologies that harness the power of energy frequencies for healing, communication, and other purposes.

To understand the 33rd Degree, it is essential to develop a deep understanding of energy frequencies. This requires a combination of intellectual knowledge and experiential understanding. We must learn to feel the vibrations of the universe, to attune ourselves to their subtle nuances, and to differentiate between the various frequencies that permeate our existence.

By doing so, we can begin to reveal the secrets of mental control over the energy field, laying the foundation for deeper exploration into the domains of the 33rd Degree.

3

Identifying Your Personal Energy Signature: Self-Discovery

"You are a unique and special being, and your energy signature reflects your individuality."

Your energy is a unique symphony, a harmonious blend of vibrations that define your essence. This unique composition is known as your personal energy signature, a cosmic fingerprint that sets you apart from all others.

Your energy signature is a complex interplay of physical, emotional, mental, and spiritual factors. It is influenced by your experiences, beliefs, and emotions, and it reflects your unique vibrational frequency.

Much like a cosmic fingerprint etched in the fabric of the universe, your energy signature is an intricate symphony of frequencies that harmonize the subtle elements of your being—physical, emotional,

IDENTIFYING YOUR PERSONAL ENERGY SIGNATURE: SELF-DISCOVERY

mental, and spiritual. Understanding and identifying this signature is essential for personal growth and mastery over the energy fields that influence your life.

To begin this exploration, it is crucial to attune your inner awareness to the delicate oscillations that comprise your energetic identity. This process starts with centering yourself in a tranquil state of meditative introspection. Find a quiet space where you can sit comfortably, free from distractions. As you breathe deeply, allow your mind to settle and your body to relax. Visualize an ethereal light enveloping your entire being, resonating with your core essence. This light symbolizes your intrinsic energy—a luminous expression woven from your experiences, emotions, and inherent qualities.

As you focus on this visualization, pay close attention to the sensations and vibrations that arise within you. These sensations serve as a guide toward understanding your unique energetic imprint. You may feel warmth radiating from your core, or perhaps a tingling sensation that dances along your skin. Each of these experiences holds significance, offering insights into the nature of your energy signature.

Next, engage in the practice of energy scanning. This technique involves running your hands a few inches above your body, sensing the subtle shifts in temperature, tingling, or pressure. These variations are indicative of your energy signature's characteristics. Observe any areas of intensity or calmness, as these sensations symbolize different aspects of your energetic state. For example, a warm, radiant sensation might signify a strong positive energy flow, while a cool, stagnant feeling could indicate blockages or imbalances within your energy field.

Trusting your intuition is paramount during this process. Your intuition acts as a compass, guiding you through the enigmatic landscape of your personal energy field. As you become more attuned to your energy signature, you may begin to notice patterns and themes that emerge. Perhaps certain emotions consistently trigger specific sensations, or you find that particular environments amplify your energy. Recognizing these patterns is essential for understanding how your energy interacts with the world around you.

The concept of energy signatures is not merely theoretical; it is grounded in the understanding that every individual emits a unique vibrational frequency. This frequency is shaped by a multitude of factors, including personal experiences, emotional states, and even physical health. Research has shown that our emotional states can significantly influence our energy signatures. For instance, emotions such as joy, love, and gratitude resonate at higher frequencies, while feelings of fear, anger, and sadness vibrate at lower frequencies.

Dr. David R. Hawkins, a renowned psychiatrist and spiritual teacher, developed a scale that assigns distinct frequency values to different emotions. His work illustrates how our emotional states can create an energy field that affects not only ourselves but also those around us. When we emit high-frequency emotions, we contribute to a positive energy environment, fostering connection and harmony. Conversely, low-frequency emotions can create discord and disconnection.

As you continue to explore your personal energy signature, it is essential to engage in practices that promote emotional awareness and regulation. Mindfulness meditation, for example, can help you cultivate a deeper understanding of your emotional landscape. By observing your thoughts and feelings without judgment, you can gain insights into how they influence your energy signature. This practice allows you to identify patterns of negativity or self-sabotage that may be holding you back from reaching your full potential.

Another valuable technique for identifying your energy signature is journaling. By documenting your thoughts, feelings, and experiences, you can begin to see correlations between your emotional states and the sensations you experience in your body. Over time, this practice can reveal the underlying themes that define your energy signature, helping you to understand how your unique vibrational patterns influence your interactions with others and the world around you.

In addition to self-reflection, consider seeking feedback from trusted friends or mentors. Sharing your experiences and insights with others can provide valuable perspectives that enhance your understanding of your energy signature. Those who know you well may be able to identify patterns or themes that you may not have recognized on your own. This collaborative approach can deepen your awareness and foster personal growth.

As you delve deeper into the process of identifying your personal energy signature, it is also essential to explore the concept of energy compatibility. Just as individuals resonate at different frequencies, we are naturally drawn to those whose energy signatures complement our own. This phenomenon is often referred to as the "law of attraction." When our energy signatures align with others, we create harmonious connections that foster growth, support, and mutual understanding.

Conversely, when we find ourselves in relationships or environments that do not resonate with our energy signature, we may experience discomfort or imbalance. Recognizing these dynamics is crucial for maintaining our energetic well-being. If you find yourself consistently feeling drained or out of sync in certain relationships, it may be a sign that your energy signature is not compatible with those around you. In such cases, it is essential to assess whether these connections serve your highest good or if it may be time to reevaluate your interactions.

Moreover, understanding your personal energy signature can empower you to make conscious choices about where to invest your time and energy. By surrounding yourself with individuals and environments that uplift and inspire you, you can cultivate a positive energy field that supports your growth and well-being. This intentional approach to relationships and environments can significantly enhance your ability to thrive.

As you continue on your journey of self-discovery, consider incorporating practices that promote energetic balance and harmony. Techniques such as yoga, tai chi, or qigong can help you cultivate awareness of your body and energy flow. These practices encourage the movement of energy within your being, facilitating the release of blockages and promoting a sense of alignment.

Additionally, engaging in creative expression—whether through art, music, or writing—can serve as a powerful outlet for your energy signature. Creative endeavors allow you to channel your unique vibrational patterns into tangible forms, fostering a deeper connection with your essence. This process not only enhances your self-awareness but also contributes to the collective energy field, as your creativity resonates with others and invites them to explore their own energy signatures.

By identifying your personal energy signature, you can gain a deeper understanding of yourself and your place in the universe. You can also learn to harness the power of your energy to create positive change in

IDENTIFYING YOUR PERSONAL ENERGY SIGNATURE: SELF-DISCOVERY

your life.

Remember, your personal energy signature is a dynamic and ever-evolving force. As you grow and evolve, your energy signature will change and adapt. By regularly tuning into your energy field, you can stay connected to your authentic self and continue to unlock your full potential.

4

Balancing Your Chakras: Harmonizing the Energy Centers

"The body is a temple, and the chakras are its sacred chambers."

As you delve deeper into the realm of energy, you will discover the intricate network of chakras that govern your holistic well-being. These energy centers, often depicted as spinning vortices of light, are located along the spine and correspond to various aspects of your physical, emotional, and spiritual existence.

When your chakras are balanced, the flow of prana, the life force that animates your being, is unobstructed. This harmonious flow promotes physical health, emotional well-being, and spiritual growth.

As you cultivate an intimate understanding of your personal energy signature, the next step is to harmonize the flow of this energy through the intricate network of chakras—essential energy centers that govern your holistic well-being. Imagine these chakras as ethereal vortices,

BALANCING YOUR CHAKRAS: HARMONIZING THE ENERGY CENTERS

each resonating with a specific frequency and color, intricately woven into the essence of your being. The alignment and balance of these chakras promote the unobstructed circulation of Prana, the life force that animates your physical and spiritual existence.

To begin this journey of chakra balancing, direct your attention to the Muladhara chakra, located at the base of your spine. This crimson vortex grounds your being, anchoring your energy to the Earth. Visualize a radiant red light pulsating with stability and security. As you focus on this energy center, allow yourself to feel its connection to the physical world, where your basic needs are met. The Muladhara chakra is foundational; when it is balanced, you experience a sense of safety and security that enables you to explore the higher aspects of your being without fear.

Next, as you move upward, encounter the Svadhisthana chakra, a vibrant orange wheel of creativity and passion located just below your navel. Envision this chakra glowing with the warmth of a setting sun, invigorating your creative essence. This energy center is closely linked to your emotions, desires, and the ability to experience pleasure. When the Svadhisthana chakra is balanced, you feel a sense of flow in your life, allowing you to express your creativity and connect with others on a deeper level. Conversely, an imbalance may manifest as creative blocks or emotional instability, which can hinder your ability to enjoy life fully.

As you ascend further, you reach the Manipura chakra, the solar plexus energy center. This luminous yellow center of power and self-will is located in the upper abdomen. Feel its golden energy emboldening your confidence and self-esteem. The Manipura chakra is often referred to as the seat of personal power, influencing your ability to take action and assert yourself in the world. When this chakra is balanced, you exude confidence and motivation, enabling you to pursue your goals with vigor. However, if it is imbalanced, you may experience feelings of powerlessness or excessive control over others, leading to conflict in relationships.

The next energy center is the Anahata chakra, located at the center of your chest and associated with the color green. This chakra emanates a soothing light that harmonizes love and compassion. When the Anahata chakra is open and balanced, you can give and receive love freely, fostering deep connections with others. It is the bridge between the lower and upper chakras, integrating your physical and spiritual experiences. An imbalance in this chakra may result in feelings of isolation, jealousy, or difficulty in forming healthy relationships. By nurturing this energy center, you cultivate a sense of empathy and understanding, allowing love to flow unimpeded.

Moving upward, you encounter the Vishuddha chakra, the throat energy center associated with communication and truth. This cerulean blue disc governs your ability to express yourself authentically. Visualize this chakra glowing brightly as you speak your truth and share your thoughts and feelings openly. When the Vishuddha chakra is balanced, you communicate with clarity and confidence, fostering healthy dialogue in your relationships. An imbalance may lead to issues such as difficulty expressing yourself, fear of speaking, or even excessive talking without substance. By focusing on this energy center, you can enhance your communication skills and build stronger connections with others.

Higher still is the Ajna chakra, commonly known as the third eye. This indigo beacon awakens intuition and insight, allowing you to perceive the world beyond the physical realm. As you concentrate on this chakra, envision a radiant light illuminating your inner vision and expanding your awareness. The Ajna chakra is essential for developing your intuitive abilities and accessing higher states of consciousness. When balanced, you experience clarity in your thoughts and a deep sense of inner knowing. Conversely, an imbalance may manifest as confusion, lack of direction, or difficulty trusting your instincts. By nurturing this energy center, you can enhance your intuitive abilities and gain deeper insights into your life's purpose.

Finally, you reach the Sahasrara chakra, the crown energy center located at the top of your head. This thousand-petaled lotus of violet light connects you to divine consciousness and universal wisdom. Visualize this chakra opening like a flower, allowing the light of higher consciousness to flow into your being. The Sahasrara chakra is the gateway to spiritual enlightenment and connection to the cosmos. When balanced, you experience a profound sense of unity with all that is, fostering spiritual growth and understanding. An imbalance in this chakra may lead to feelings of disconnection from your spiritual path or a lack of purpose in life. By focusing on this energy center, you can cultivate a deeper connection to the divine and enhance your spiritual journey.

The process of balancing your chakras involves deliberate intention and visualization. As you work through each energy center, take the time to connect with the unique qualities and attributes associated with each chakra. Use affirmations, meditation, and breathwork to reinforce your intentions for balance and harmony. For instance, when working with the Muladhara chakra, you might affirm, "I am grounded and secure in my being." As you repeat this affirmation, visualize the radiant red light pulsating at the base of your spine, anchoring you to the Earth.

Incorporating movement into your chakra balancing practice can also be beneficial. Engaging in yoga poses that correspond to each chakra can help release stagnant energy and promote flow. For the Muladhara chakra, consider grounding poses such as Mountain Pose or Warrior I. For the Svadhisthana chakra, hip-opening poses like Pigeon Pose can help stimulate creativity and passion. The Manipura chakra can be activated through core-strengthening poses like Boat Pose, while heart-opening poses such as Cobra or Camel can enhance the energy of the Anahata chakra. The Vishuddha chakra can be supported by poses that open the throat, such as Fish Pose, while the Ajna chakra can be stimulated through seated forward bends that promote introspection. Finally, the Sahasrara chakra can be enhanced through meditation and poses that encourage stillness, such as Child's Pose.

In addition to yoga, consider incorporating breathwork into your practice. Breath is a powerful tool for energy movement and can help clear blockages in your chakras. Techniques such as alternate nostril breathing can promote balance and harmony throughout your energy centers. As you practice, visualize the breath flowing through each chakra, cleansing and revitalizing the energy within.

Sound healing is another effective method for balancing chakras. Each chakra resonates with a specific frequency and can be activated through sound vibrations. You can use singing bowls, tuning forks, or even your voice to create sounds that correspond to each chakra. For example, the Muladhara chakra resonates with the note C, while the Svadhisthana chakra resonates with D. By incorporating sound into your practice, you can enhance the vibrational qualities of each energy center, promoting deeper healing and balance.

As you embark on this journey of chakra balancing, remember that it is an ongoing process. Your energy centers may shift and change in response to your life experiences, emotions, and personal growth. Regularly checking in with your chakras and practicing techniques to maintain balance can help you cultivate a harmonious flow of energy in your life.

Pay attention to the signs of imbalance in your chakras. Physical symptoms such as tension, pain, or fatigue may indicate that a particular energy center requires attention. Emotional disturbances, such as anxiety, anger, or sadness, can also signal that a chakra is out of balance. By recognizing these signs, you can take proactive steps to restore harmony and well-being.

Creating a supportive environment for your chakra balancing practice is essential. Surround yourself with elements that resonate with the energy of each chakra. For example, incorporating the colors associated with each energy center into your space can help reinforce their qualities. You might use red decor to support the Muladhara chakra, orange elements for the Svadhisthana chakra, and so on. Additionally, incorporating natural elements such as plants, crystals, and essential oils can enhance the energetic atmosphere of your space.

By focusing on these chakras and visualizing their energy, you can begin to cultivate a symphony of balanced energy. This harmonious flow will promote physical health, emotional well-being, and spiritual growth.

5

Developing Intuition Through Meditation: Tapping into the Wisdom Within

"Meditation is the art of listening to the silence within."

Intuition, a subtle yet powerful force, is often described as a sixth sense. It is the ability to perceive information without the use of conscious thought or reasoning. While intuition can sometimes seem mysterious or inexplicable, it is actually a natural part of our being, a connection to a deeper level of consciousness.

Meditation is a powerful tool for developing intuition. By quieting the mind and connecting with your inner self, you can create the space necessary for intuitive insights to emerge.

Accessing the depths of your intuitive faculties begins with the profound practice of meditation, where the boundaries between the conscious

DEVELOPING INTUITION THROUGH MEDITATION: TAPPING INTO THE...

mind and higher wisdom dissolve into a seamless flow of insight and clarity. This sacred practice, when undertaken with genuine intent, allows you to traverse the realms where intuitive knowledge resides. Meditation serves as a conduit, harmonizing the vibrational frequencies of your psyche with universal consciousness, enabling you to perceive truths that lie beyond the veil of ordinary perception.

To commence this journey, it is essential to create a sanctified space devoid of distractions. Find a quiet corner in your home or a serene outdoor setting where you can sit comfortably without interruptions. As you settle into this space, relax your body and mind. Close your eyes and concentrate on your breathing. With each inhale, visualize a luminous energy spiraling through your chakras, aligning them in a symphony of resonance. This alignment is crucial as it primes your energy field for deeper intuitive reception.

As you breathe deeply, allow your mind to focus on the sensations within your body. With each breath, feel the air filling your lungs, expanding your chest, and nourishing your entire being. This practice of mindful breathing not only calms your mind but also enhances your ability to connect with your inner self. The more you practice this focused breathing, the more you will find that your thoughts begin to settle, creating a fertile ground for intuitive insights to emerge.

Next, invoke a state of heightened awareness by directing your focus inward. Envision a radiant light emanating from your third eye, the seat of intuition located between your eyebrows. This light represents your connection to higher consciousness and your intuitive faculties. Allow this illumination to permeate your entire being, filling you with a sense of peace and clarity. As you maintain this focus, you may begin to experience subtle shifts in your perceptual field—fleeting images, symbolic patterns, or ephemeral sounds. These are the whispers of your inner wisdom, the echoes of the cosmic symphony.

Remain in this meditative state, allowing these intuitive impressions to crystallize within your consciousness. It is essential to be patient during this process. Intuition often speaks in gentle nudges rather than loud proclamations. As you cultivate this practice, you may find that insights arise unexpectedly, guiding you toward decisions or revelations that resonate deeply with your inner truth.

Recording any insights that surface is crucial, no matter how enigmatic they may seem. Keep a journal dedicated to your intuitive experiences. Write down your thoughts, feelings, and any images or symbols that arise during meditation. Over time, you will begin to notice patterns and themes in your intuitive messages, enhancing your ability to discern and interpret these insights. This practice of documentation not only reinforces your connection to your intuition but also serves as a valuable reference for future reflection.

With consistent practice, you will refine your ability to discern and interpret these intuitive messages, cultivating a profound connection with the universal energy field. As you deepen your meditation practice, consider incorporating various techniques to enhance your intuitive abilities. Mindfulness meditation, for instance, encourages you to observe your thoughts and feelings without judgment, helping you become more aware of your intuitive insights as they arise.

Another powerful technique is guided visualization, where you can create mental scenarios that allow your intuition to guide you through them. This method can be particularly effective in decision-making processes. By visualizing potential outcomes and allowing your intuition to inform your choices, you can develop a stronger sense of clarity and direction in your life.

Third eye meditation is another effective practice for enhancing intuition. By focusing on the area between your eyebrows, you can activate this energy center associated with intuition and spiritual insight. As you meditate, visualize a single point of light expanding and connecting you to your higher self. This practice can help you tap into your innate wisdom and enhance your intuitive abilities.

Loving-kindness meditation is also valuable for cultivating compassion and empathy, which can deepen your connection to your intuition. By sending love and kindness to yourself and others, you foster a sense of interconnectedness that enhances your intuitive insights. This practice encourages you to listen to your inner voice with compassion, allowing your intuition to guide you in your interactions with others.

Incorporating yoga into your meditation practice can further enhance your intuitive development. Yoga combines physical movement with mindfulness, creating a holistic approach that fosters a deeper connection with your inner self. As you practice yoga, pay attention to how your body feels in each pose. This heightened awareness can help you tune into your intuition and recognize the subtle signals your body sends you.

As you explore these various meditation techniques, remember that developing intuition is a deeply personal journey. Each individual may resonate with different practices, so it is essential to find what works best for you. Experiment with different techniques and observe how they impact your intuitive insights. Trust your instincts as you navigate this process, allowing your intuition to guide you toward the practices that resonate most.

Research has shown that meditation can significantly enhance intuitive abilities. Studies indicate that regular meditation practice increases activity in the prefrontal cortex, the part of the brain associated with higher cognitive functions such as decision-making, problem-solving, and intuition. Long-term meditators often report a greater ability to make accurate intuitive decisions compared to non-meditators. This connection between meditation and intuition underscores the importance of cultivating a consistent meditation practice.

As you continue to develop your intuition through meditation, you may encounter moments of doubt or uncertainty. It is natural to question your intuitive insights, especially if they challenge your logical reasoning. However, learning to trust your intuition is a vital aspect of this journey. Intuition often operates outside the realm of logic, tapping into a deeper understanding that transcends rational thought. By cultivating a sense of trust in your intuitive faculties, you empower yourself to make decisions that align with your authentic self.

To further enhance your intuitive practice, consider joining a meditation group or seeking guidance from experienced practitioners. Engaging with others who share similar interests can provide valuable insights and support as you navigate your intuitive journey. Group meditation sessions can also amplify the collective energy, creating a powerful environment for intuitive growth.

In addition to formal meditation practices, integrating mindfulness into your daily life can significantly enhance your intuitive abilities. Pay attention to the subtle cues and sensations that arise throughout your day. Whether it's a gut feeling about a decision or a sudden insight while in conversation, being present and aware of these moments can deepen your connection to your intuition.

As you cultivate this awareness, you may find that your intuition becomes more pronounced in your everyday life. You might experience moments of clarity that guide your decisions, or you may develop a heightened sensitivity to the energies of those around you. This increased awareness can enrich your relationships and enhance your ability to navigate complex situations with grace and confidence.

Ultimately, the practice of meditation serves as a powerful tool for developing intuition. By creating a sacred space for introspection and insight, you can access the depths of your inner wisdom and cultivate a profound connection to the universal energy field.

6

Decoding Energy Patterns: The Cosmic Symphony

"The universe is a symphony of vibrations, and we are all playing our part."

To decode the intricate patterns of energy that shape our reality, we must immerse ourselves in the cosmic symphony. This symphony is composed of countless vibrations, each contributing to the grand tapestry of existence.

The ancient maxim "as above, so below" suggests that the patterns of the cosmos are reflected in our earthly existence. By observing the celestial rhythms and terrestrial vibrations, we can begin to discern the underlying order of the universe.

One of the most fundamental concepts in understanding energy patterns is the concept of cycles. Everything in the universe operates in cycles, from the rotation of the Earth to the ebb and flow of the tides. These cycles are not arbitrary; they are reflections of the underlying cosmic order.

By studying these cycles, we can gain valuable insights into the nature of energy and its influence on our lives.

Begin by observing the recurring symbols and anomalies within these patterns. The Fibonacci sequence, for instance, is a mathematical pattern found in various natural phenomena, including the arrangement of leaves on a stem, the branching of trees, and even the spirals of galaxies. This sequence illustrates how nature adheres to specific ratios and proportions, creating a sense of harmony and balance.

The golden ratio, another intriguing mathematical concept, can be observed in the human form, the proportions of ancient architecture, and the patterns of seashells. By contemplating these symbols, we begin to discern the underlying order of the universe, a testament to the interconnectedness of all things.

Shift your focus to the ebb and flow of natural cycles—seasons, lunar phases, and tidal movements. These cycles are the Earth's heartbeat, a reflection of the cosmic pulse that governs our existence. By synchronizing your activities and thoughts with these natural rhythms, you'll find yourself in harmony with the greater energy field. Imagine yourself as a leaf, gently swaying in the breeze, adapting to the changing seasons and the cycle of day and night. This connection with the natural world not only grounds you in the present moment but also reminds you of your place within the grand tapestry of life.

Delve deeper by exploring the concept of chakras and meridians within your own body. These energy centers and pathways are microcosms of the universal energy grid, reflecting the intricate patterns that govern the cosmos. Through meditative practices, you can tune into these internal patterns, allowing you to decode the energy imprints within and around you. Visualize your chakras as glowing orbs of light, each vibrating at a unique frequency and color, aligning to form a luminous column of energy. As you focus on these centers, you may experience sensations of warmth, tingling, or a sense of expansion, all of which are indicators of the flow of energy within your being.

To further enhance your understanding of energy patterns, consider the concept of sacred geometry. The Flower of Life, for example, is a geometric figure composed of multiple overlapping circles, symbolizing the rhythm and patterns inherent in the universe. Each shape within the Flower of Life reflects unique vibrational frequencies, akin to musical notes in a grand symphony, reminding us of the harmonious structure that governs our existence. By contemplating these geometric forms, we attune ourselves to the universal principles that underpin reality, allowing us to align our energy with the rhythms of the cosmos.

As you continue to explore the world of energy patterns, remember that this journey is not merely an intellectual exercise; it is a deeply experiential process that requires you to engage with your senses and intuition. Trust your gut feelings, your dreams, and your synchronistic experiences, for they are all manifestations of the energy field that surrounds and permeates your being. Keep a journal of your observations, your insights, and your questions, for they will serve as a roadmap on your journey of self-discovery.

Ultimately, decoding energy patterns requires a blend of intuitive insight and empirical observation. It is a journey of aligning your inner frequencies with the cosmic symphony, enabling you to navigate the complexities of existence with heightened awareness and control. As you delve deeper into this exploration, remember that you are not merely a passive observer; you are an active participant in the grand dance of energy that defines our universe.

In the words of the renowned physicist Nikola Tesla, "If you want to find the secrets of the universe, think in terms of energy, frequency, and vibration." By embracing this perspective and engaging with the energy patterns that surround us, we unlock the keys to understanding the fundamental nature of reality. We become conductors in the orchestra of life, attuning our energy to the rhythms of the cosmos and harnessing the power of the universal energy field to create the life we desire.

Decoding energy patterns requires a blend of intuitive insight and empirical observation. It is a journey of aligning our inner frequencies with the cosmic symphony, enabling us to navigate the complexities of existence with heightened awareness and control.

By understanding the patterns of energy that shape our reality, we can gain a deeper appreciation for the interconnectedness of all things. We can also learn to harness the power of these patterns to create positive change in our lives and the world around us.

7

The Power of Resonance and Vibration: Harmonizing with the Cosmic Symphony

"Everything is vibration. Everything in the universe vibrates at a specific frequency."

The universe is a symphony of vibrations, a harmonious interplay of frequencies that shape the fabric of reality. Every thought, emotion, and action sends ripples through this cosmic orchestra, influencing and being influenced by the surrounding energy fields.

To understand the power of resonance and vibration, we must first grasp the concept of frequency. Frequency is the rate at which something vibrates. Everything in the universe vibrates at a specific frequency, from atoms to galaxies.

When two objects vibrate at the same frequency, they are said to be in resonance. Resonance is a powerful phenomenon that can amplify vibrations and create a harmonious interaction between objects.

In the realm of energy, resonance is not merely a physical phenomenon; it is a sacred alignment of frequencies that can realign your inner and outer worlds. By attuning yourself to specific vibrational frequencies, you can channel the primordial forces that govern existence.

Resonance acts as a bridge, connecting your consciousness with the universal symphony. It is not just about hearing a sound or feeling a pulse; it is about becoming one with the oscillations that permeate the ether.

By attuning yourself to specific vibrational frequencies, you channel the primordial forces that govern existence. Resonance acts as a bridge, connecting your consciousness with the universal symphony. It's not just about hearing a sound or feeling a pulse; it's about becoming one with the oscillations that permeate the ether. Imagine yourself as a tuning fork in the grand orchestra of the universe. When struck, your frequencies resonate, harmonizing with the surrounding energy fields. This resonance amplifies your mental control over the energy field, enabling you to mold and shape it with intention. Symbolically, think of it as tuning into the divine frequency that orchestrates the cosmos.

Consider the ancient wisdom of sacred geometries and cymatics, where sound waves create intricate patterns in matter. These visual manifestations of resonance reveal the hidden order and unity within the chaos of the material world. When you align your mind with these sacred vibrations, you tap into the underlying structure of reality itself. The Flower of Life, for instance, is a geometric figure composed of multiple overlapping circles, symbolizing the rhythm and patterns inherent in the universe. Each shape within the Flower of Life reflects unique vibrational frequencies, akin to musical notes in a grand symphony, reminding us of the harmonious structure that governs our existence.

To harness the power of resonance and vibration, you must cultivate a deep awareness of your own energetic state. Through meditative practices and intentional focus, you can synchronize your vibration with the higher frequencies, achieving greater control over the energy field. This mastery isn't just a skill but a profound journey into the heart of cosmic harmony.

Imagine a tuning fork, struck with precision, sending out a pure, resonant tone. As the vibrations travel through the air, they encounter another tuning fork, identical in size and shape. The second tuning fork, sensing the resonant frequency of the first, begins to vibrate in sympathy, amplifying the original sound. This is the essence of resonance – the ability of one vibrating system to influence another, causing it to oscillate at the same frequency.

In the realm of energy and consciousness, this principle holds true on a cosmic scale. Every thought, emotion, and intention we send out into the universe is a vibration, a frequency that interacts with the vast web of energy that permeates all existence. When we align our vibrations with the higher frequencies of love, compassion, and unity, we create a resonance that amplifies these qualities, drawing them to us and influencing the world around us.

Conversely, when we resonate with lower frequencies of fear, anger, or negativity, we become trapped in a cycle of disharmony, attracting more of the same into our lives. It is through the conscious cultivation of higher vibrational states that we can harness the power of resonance to transform ourselves and our world.

One of the most powerful tools for aligning our vibrations with the higher frequencies is the practice of meditation. Through the stillness and focus of meditation, we can quiet the chatter of the mind and attune ourselves to the subtle rhythms of the universe. As we breathe deeply and let go of our attachments, we begin to resonate with the eternal now, the timeless present moment that is the foundation of all existence.

In this state of resonance, we tap into the wellspring of creativity and insight that lies at the heart of the cosmos. Ideas and solutions that once seemed elusive now flow freely, as we align our consciousness with the infinite intelligence that permeates all things. We become channels for the divine, conduits for the creative power that shapes reality itself.

But the power of resonance is not limited to the inner realm of consciousness; it also manifests in the physical world around us. The ancient science of cymatics, pioneered by scientists like Hans Jenny, has revealed the stunning patterns that emerge when sound waves interact with physical matter. By vibrating a metal plate covered in sand or liquid, Jenny was able to create intricate geometric forms that mirrored the frequencies of the sound waves.

These patterns, known as Chladni figures, are not merely aesthetic curiosities; they are visual representations of the underlying order that governs the universe. They show us that every vibration, every frequency, has a corresponding form, a unique signature that is etched into the fabric of reality. By understanding and working with these patterns, we can tap into the fundamental building blocks of creation itself.

The implications of this knowledge are profound. If every thought and intention is a vibration that interacts with the energy field, then we have the power to shape our reality through the conscious cultivation of higher frequencies. By aligning our minds and hearts with the frequencies of love, abundance, and well-being, we can create a resonance that attracts these qualities into our lives. We become co-creators with the universe, shaping the world around us with the power of our focused intention.

But this power comes with responsibility. As we deepen our understanding of resonance and vibration, we must also cultivate a sense of reverence and respect for the sacred nature of creation. We are not separate from the universe; we are an integral part of it, and our actions have consequences that ripple out into the world. By aligning our vibrations with the higher frequencies of compassion and service, we can create a resonance that uplifts all of humanity, and perhaps even the entire planet.

In this way, the power of resonance and vibration is not just about personal transformation; it is about collective transformation, about creating a world that works for everyone. It is about recognizing our interconnectedness, our oneness with all that is, and using that knowledge to create a better future for all. It is about tapping into the infinite potential of the universe and channeling it through our own unique gifts and talents, to make a positive difference in the world.

8

Harmonizing with the Universal Field: Becoming a Conduit for Cosmic Energy

"We are all connected to everything else in the universe."

The universe is a vast interconnected web of energy, a cosmic symphony that binds all living and non-living entities together. This intricate tapestry, often referred to as the universal or quantum field, is the source of all creation.

To harmonize with the universal field, we must first embrace the profound interconnectedness that underlies all existence. This requires a deep comprehension of the vibrational frequencies that permeate the cosmos.

By attuning ourselves to these universal frequencies, we can reveal the latent potential of our own energetic blueprint. We can become conduits for cosmic energy, channeling the power of the universe through our own being.

Begin by cultivating an awareness of the subtle vibrations and oscillations that flow through and around you. These vibrations are not merely background noise; they are the very fabric of reality, shaping your experiences and interactions. Meditative practices such as mindful breathwork and visualization serve as essential tools in aligning your personal energy with these cosmic frequencies. As you engage in these practices, envision yourself as a conduit, a vessel through which universal energy courses, harmonizing your being with the greater whole.

To deepen this connection, engage in activities that amplify your sensitivity to these energies. Chanting mantras, for instance, can elevate your vibrational state and align your energy with the universal field. The sound of your voice, resonating with specific frequencies, creates a ripple effect that extends beyond your physical body, influencing the energy around you. Similarly, employing sacred geometry can enhance your understanding of the patterns that govern the universe. By visualizing these geometric shapes, you tap into the underlying principles of creation, aligning your energy with the cosmic order.

Crystals, known for their resonant properties, can also serve as powerful allies in your journey toward harmonization. Each crystal vibrates at a unique frequency, and by working with specific stones, you can amplify your energy and align with the universal field. For example, clear quartz is known for its ability to enhance clarity and amplify intentions, while amethyst promotes spiritual awareness and connection to higher realms. By incorporating these tools into your practice, you create a harmonious environment that supports your energetic alignment.

Remember that harmonizing with the universal field is not a one-time event but a continuous, evolving process. It demands persistent dedication to self-awareness and an unwavering commitment to spiritual growth. As you progress on this journey, you will find that your ability to influence and manipulate energy fields becomes more intuitive and fluid. This state of harmonic convergence allows you to transcend the constraints of the physical sphere, paving the way for higher states of consciousness and a more thorough comprehension of the spiritual realm.

In this context, consider the concept of resonance, which plays a crucial role in your ability to harmonize with the universal field. Resonance occurs when an object or system vibrates at the same frequency as another, creating a powerful amplification of energy. This phenomenon can be observed in nature, such as when a singer hits a note that causes a glass to shatter. The glass resonates with the frequency of the note, resulting in a dramatic effect. Similarly, when you align your personal energy with the frequencies of the universe, you amplify your ability to co-create reality.

As you cultivate this resonance, you may begin to notice shifts in your perception and experience. You might find that you are more attuned to the subtle energies around you, able to sense the emotional states of others or the underlying currents of a situation. This heightened awareness allows you to navigate your interactions with greater ease and intention, fostering deeper connections and more harmonious relationships.

To further enhance your ability to harmonize with the universal field, consider the practice of gratitude. Gratitude is a powerful vibrational frequency that can elevate your energy and align you with the abundance of the universe. By regularly expressing gratitude for the blessings in your life, you create a resonance that attracts more positive experiences. This practice not only enhances your personal energy but also contributes to the collective energy of the universe, fostering a sense of unity and interconnectedness.

In addition to gratitude, cultivating compassion and empathy can deepen your connection to the universal field. When you approach others with an open heart and a willingness to understand their experiences, you create a resonance that fosters healing and connection. This compassionate energy ripples outward, influencing the collective consciousness and contributing to a more harmonious world.

As you continue to explore the depths of your connection to the universal field, it is essential to remain open to the lessons and insights that arise along the way. Each experience, whether perceived as positive or negative, offers an opportunity for growth and understanding. By embracing these lessons with an open mind and heart, you can navigate the complexities of existence with grace and ease.

Engaging in regular self-reflection can also support your journey toward harmonization. Take time to assess your thoughts, emotions, and actions, considering how they align with your intention to connect with the universal field. Journaling can be a powerful tool for this process, allowing you to articulate your insights and track your progress over time. As you reflect on your experiences, you may uncover patterns or themes that reveal deeper truths about your energetic state and your relationship with the universe.

Incorporating movement into your practice can further enhance your ability to harmonize with the universal field. Activities such as yoga, tai chi, or dance allow you to express your energy physically, creating a dynamic flow that aligns your body, mind, and spirit. These practices not only promote physical well-being but also facilitate the release of stagnant energy, allowing for a more fluid connection to the universal field.

As you cultivate this harmonious connection, you may find that your intuition becomes more pronounced. Your ability to sense the subtle energies around you will deepen, allowing you to navigate your experiences with greater clarity and confidence. This intuitive guidance can serve as a compass, helping you make decisions that align with your highest self and your purpose in the world.

In this process, remember that you are not alone. The universe is a vast and supportive network of energies, and as you align with the universal field, you tap into this collective wisdom. Trust in the guidance that emerges from your connection to the cosmos, and allow it to inform your choices and actions.

As you progress, you will find that your ability to influence and manipulate energy fields becomes more intuitive and fluid. In this state of harmonic convergence, you are not merely coexisting with the universe; you are actively participating in its perpetual dance.

You are co-creating reality through the symphonic interplay of energy frequencies. Your ability to transcend the constraints of the physical sphere is made possible by this fundamental alignment, which also paves the way for higher states of consciousness and a more profound understanding of the spiritual realm.

By harmonizing with the universal field, you become a vessel for divine energy, a conduit for the infinite potential of the cosmos.

9

Sensing and Reading Energy Fields: Becoming a Master of Vibrational Perception

"There's an everlasting symphony of vibrations, resonate with it."

As you deepen your resonance with the universal field, your next endeavor is to master the art of sensing and reading energy fields. This profound skill demands an acute attunement to the subtle currents that permeate all matter and consciousness. To begin this journey, cultivate a meditative state where your mind is both vigilant and serene. In this heightened awareness, you will perceive the ebbs and flows of energetic frequencies, akin to the ripples in a still pond responding to a gentle breeze.

Initiate your practice by focusing on your own energy field. Visualize it as a luminous aura pulsating with your life force. This aura is not merely a visual phenomenon; it is a dynamic representation of your emotional, mental, and spiritual states. As you extend your perception outward, feel the interplay between your energy and the ambient field around you. Notice variations in density, texture, and warmth. These fluctuations are the signatures of different energetic entities and states, revealing the intricate dance of energy that surrounds you.

As your sensitivity increases, you will start to decode the symbolic language of energy. For instance, a sudden coolness may signify an influx of calming vibrations, while a warm surge could indicate heightened emotional or physical activity. Trust your intuitive impressions; they are the keys to discovering a deeper understanding of the energetic landscape. Engaging with nature can further enhance your ability to sense and read energy fields. Nature presents a symphony of pure, unadulterated frequencies that can sharpen your perception.

Consider placing your hands on a tree, feeling its grounding energy merge with yours. Trees are remarkable conduits of energy, often acting as stabilizers in our energetic environment. As you connect with the tree, visualize its roots extending deep into the Earth, drawing up nourishing energy that flows into your being. This practice will sharpen your ability to distinguish between various energetic qualities and sources, enhancing your overall sensitivity to the energy fields that surround you.

As you progress in your ability to sense energy, it is essential to cultivate a mindset of curiosity and openness. Approach each experience with the intention to learn and understand, rather than to judge or categorize. This openness allows you to perceive the subtleties of energy without the interference of preconceived notions or biases.

To further refine your skills, consider engaging in exercises that promote energy sensitivity. One effective method is to practice with a partner. Sit facing each other and take a few moments to ground yourself through deep breathing. Once you feel centered, close your eyes and extend your awareness outward. Ask your partner to send energy toward you without physical contact. Pay attention to the sensations that arise in your body—do you feel warmth, tingling, or perhaps a gentle pull? This exercise helps you develop your ability to discern different energy signatures and enhances your confidence in your intuitive abilities.

Another valuable practice is to observe the energy dynamics in various environments. Pay attention to how your energy shifts in different settings—whether in a bustling café, a serene park, or a crowded event. Notice how the energy of the space influences your emotions and physical sensations. This awareness will deepen your understanding of how energy fields interact and how they can affect your own energetic state.

As you continue to hone your skills in sensing and reading energy fields, you may begin to notice patterns in your experiences. For example, you might find that certain individuals consistently emit a particular energy that resonates with you, while others may feel draining or uncomfortable. Recognizing these patterns is crucial for developing your intuitive abilities and understanding the dynamics of your interactions with others.

In addition to personal interactions, consider exploring the energy fields of collective environments. Group settings, such as workshops or social gatherings, create a unique energetic atmosphere. Observe how the collective energy shifts as different individuals contribute their vibrations to the space. This practice will enhance your ability to read the energy of groups and understand the dynamics at play within them.

As you deepen your connection to energy fields, it is essential to remain grounded and centered. The ability to sense and read energy can be overwhelming at times, especially if you are sensitive to the emotions and energies of others. Establishing a grounding practice, such as spending time in nature, practicing mindfulness, or engaging in physical activities, will help you maintain balance and clarity as you navigate the energetic landscape.

Developing a strong foundation of self-awareness is also crucial. Understanding your own energy patterns and emotional states will enable you to differentiate between your feelings and those of others. Regular self-reflection, journaling, and meditation can help you cultivate this awareness, allowing you to approach energy reading with a clear and open mind.

As you progress on this journey, you may also wish to explore the concept of auras. Auras are the energy fields that surround living beings, often reflecting their emotional and spiritual states. Learning to perceive and interpret auras can enhance your ability to read energy fields and deepen your understanding of the subtle dynamics at play in your interactions with others.

To practice reading auras, begin by focusing on a person you know well. As you engage in conversation, soften your gaze and allow your peripheral vision to take in the space around them. You may begin to notice subtle colors or fluctuations in the energy surrounding them.

Each color can hold specific meanings—warm colors like red and orange may indicate strong emotions or vitality, while cooler colors like blue and green may suggest calmness or healing energy.

As you develop your skills in reading energy fields, remember that this practice is not solely about interpretation; it is also about connection. The more you engage with the energies around you, the more you will cultivate a sense of empathy and understanding for the experiences of others. This connection can foster deeper relationships and enhance your ability to support those around you.

In addition to personal practice, consider seeking guidance from experienced practitioners or teachers. Workshops, classes, or mentorship programs can provide valuable insights and techniques to enhance your skills in sensing and reading energy fields. Learning from others can also help you refine your intuitive abilities and deepen your understanding of the energetic dynamics at play in various situations.

10

Shielding Yourself from Negative Energy: Protecting Your Aura

"You are the master of your own destiny, and you have the power to shield yourself from negative energy."

Harnessing the power of shielding techniques empowers you to deflect negative energies, ensuring your auric field remains untainted and resilient against external disturbances.

Envision a luminous shield and aetheric armor enveloping your entire being. This shield isn't mere imagination; it is a construct of your will, a manifestation of your psychic intent. By engaging with the vibrational frequencies within your core, you can project them outward to form a radiant barrier that oscillates with your inner light.

To initiate this process, enter a meditative state where your mind is both vigilant and serene. In this heightened awareness, you will begin to perceive the subtle energy flows around you, akin to the ripples in a still pond responding to a gentle breeze. This state of meditation allows you to center your consciousness on your heart chakra, the fulcrum of your energetic essence. Visualize a vortex of pure energy spiraling outward, forming a protective sphere around you. This sphere, imbued with your soul's frequency, serves as a sentinel, discerning and repelling malevolent entities or discordant vibrations.

Incorporating sacred symbols and ancient sigils into your shield can further enhance its potency. Symbols like the pentacle or the ankh can be visualized at the cardinal points of your shield, fortifying its effectiveness. These symbols act as cosmic keys, accessing higher vibrational states and amplifying your protective barriers. The act of visualization is not just a mental exercise; it is a powerful tool that allows you to shape your energetic environment consciously.

Chanting mantras or affirmations can also solidify this energetic defense, infusing your shield with harmonic resonance. The sound vibrations created by these mantras resonate with your energy field, reinforcing your protective barrier. As you chant, focus on the intention behind your words, allowing the vibrations to penetrate your aura and strengthen your shield. This practice not only enhances your protection but also aligns your energy with the higher frequencies of love and light.

Understanding the nature of negative energy is crucial in developing effective shielding techniques. Negative energy can manifest from various sources, including individuals, environments, and even your own thoughts. It often presents itself as feelings of heaviness, discomfort, or unease. By recognizing these signs, you can take proactive measures to shield yourself from their influence.

One effective method for shielding is to create a mental image of a protective bubble surrounding you. This bubble can be visualized as a vibrant color that resonates with your energy. For example, you might choose a bright white light or a deep blue hue, depending on what feels most protective to you. As you visualize this bubble, imagine it growing larger and more resilient with each breath you take. See it absorbing any negative energy that comes your way, transforming it into positive vibrations before it can penetrate your aura.

Additionally, grounding techniques can enhance your shielding practice. Grounding connects you to the Earth's energy, providing stability and strength. To ground yourself, visualize roots extending from your feet into the Earth, anchoring you firmly in place. As you connect with the Earth's energy, imagine it rising up through your body, filling you with a sense of security and resilience. This grounding energy acts as a buffer against negative influences, reinforcing your protective shield.

Engaging with nature is another powerful way to strengthen your shielding techniques. Nature presents a symphony of pure, unadulterated frequencies that can sharpen your ability to sense and read energy fields. Spend time outdoors, allowing the natural world to replenish your energy and reinforce your protective barriers. Place your hands on a tree, feeling its grounding energy merge with yours. Trees are remarkable conduits of energy, often acting as stabilizers in our energetic environment. As you connect with the tree, visualize its roots extending deep into the Earth, drawing up nourishing energy that flows into your being.

In addition to these practices, maintaining a positive mindset is essential for effective shielding. Your thoughts and emotions play a significant role in shaping your energy field. By cultivating a mindset of positivity and resilience, you can enhance your ability to deflect negative energies. Engage in practices that promote mental well-being, such as gratitude, mindfulness, and self-compassion. These practices not only strengthen your energy but also create a buffer against external negativity.

It's important to recognize that shielding is not about creating walls that isolate you from the world. Instead, it is about establishing a protective barrier that allows you to engage with your environment while maintaining your energetic integrity. This balance enables you to navigate the complexities of life without becoming overwhelmed by the energies of others.

As you refine your shielding techniques, you may encounter situations that challenge your ability to maintain your protective barriers. In these moments, it is crucial to remember that you have the power to recalibrate your energy. If you find yourself in a negative environment or interacting with a challenging individual, take a moment to center yourself. Breathe deeply, and visualize your protective shield expanding and strengthening around you. This conscious act of recalibration allows you to reclaim your energy and reinforce your defenses.

Another effective strategy for shielding yourself from negative energy is to practice energetic cleansing. Regularly cleansing your aura helps to remove any accumulated negativity and restore your energetic balance. There are various methods for energetic cleansing, including smudging with sage or other herbs, bathing in saltwater, or using sound vibrations from singing bowls or bells. Choose the method that resonates most with you and incorporate it into your routine.

In addition to cleansing, consider incorporating protective crystals into your shielding practice. Crystals such as black tourmaline, amethyst, and selenite are known for their protective properties. Carry these crystals with you or place them in your living space to create a shield against negative energies. As you work with these stones, set the intention for them to enhance your energetic protection, allowing their vibrations to amplify your own.

When your aura is protected, you will feel more grounded, centered, and empowered. You will be able to navigate the challenges of life with greater resilience and clarity.

So, take the time to shield yourself from negative energy. It is a powerful investment in your well-being and spiritual growth.

11

Amplifying Intentions with Visualization: Manifesting Your Desires

"The mind is a powerful tool. When used correctly, it can create miracles."

Visualization is a powerful technique that can amplify your intentions and manifest your deepest desires. By deliberately directing your mental imagery, you can imbue your energy field with vibrational frequencies that align with your aspirations.

This process is not merely about seeing; it is about perceiving with every sense, forging a vivid internal landscape in which your goals are already realized.

Through the alchemy of focused visualization, you can magnify your intentions, transmuting mere thoughts into powerful catalysts for manifesting your deepest desires. This transformative process involves deliberately directing your mental imagery, which imbues your energy field with vibrational frequencies that align with your aspirations. Visualization is not just about seeing; it is about perceiving with every sense, forging a vivid internal landscape in which your goals are already realized.

Begin by finding a quiet, sacred space where you can center your mind. This space should be free from distractions, allowing you to focus entirely on your inner experience. Once settled, close your eyes and take deep, rhythmic breaths, grounding yourself in the present moment. As you breathe, visualize a radiant light emanating from your core, expanding to envelop your entire being. This light represents your inner power, your connection to the universal energy matrix that surrounds us all.

Next, crystallize your intention. Picture it in meticulous detail. For example, if your goal is to cultivate peace, envision serene scenes: tranquil waters, gentle breezes, and calming sounds. Imagine the sensation of peace permeating your very essence. Infuse this imagery with emotion; feel the tranquility as if it were already part of you. The intensity of the energy you send into the universe is proportional to the vividness and emotional intensity of your visualization session.

As you maintain this focus, silently affirm your intention. Use affirmations that resonate deeply with you, such as "I am a vessel of peace" or "Harmony flows through me." These affirmations act as vibrational anchors, solidifying your intention within the energetic fabric of your being. The repetition of these affirmations, combined with your visualization, creates a powerful synergy that amplifies your intentions and aligns them with the universal energies.

The science behind visualization and intention-setting is supported by various studies that highlight the brain's capacity to influence reality through focused thought. Research has shown that mental imagery can activate the same neural pathways as actual experiences, suggesting that the mind does not differentiate between real and imagined events. This phenomenon underscores the significance of visualization as a tool for manifesting desires and achieving goals.

To enhance your visualization practice, consider incorporating sensory details into your mental imagery. Engage all of your senses: what do you see, hear, feel, smell, and taste in your envisioned scenario? The more vivid and immersive your visualization, the more effectively you can transmit your intentions into the universe. For instance, if you are visualizing a peaceful beach, imagine the sound of waves gently lapping at the shore, the warmth of the sun on your skin, and the scent of salt in the air. This multi-sensory approach creates a more profound impact on your subconscious mind, reinforcing your intentions.

Another vital aspect of amplifying intentions through visualization is to cultivate a state of gratitude. Gratitude is a powerful vibrational frequency that aligns you with abundance and positivity. As you visualize your intentions, take a moment to express gratitude for what you already have and for the manifestation of your desires. This practice shifts your energy from lack to abundance, creating a fertile ground for your intentions to flourish.

In addition to gratitude, maintaining a positive mindset is essential for effective visualization. Your thoughts and beliefs influence your ability to manifest your desires. If you hold limiting beliefs or negative thoughts, they can create energetic blockages that hinder your progress. Therefore, it is crucial to identify and release any self-doubt or negative self-talk that may arise during your visualization practice. Replace these limiting beliefs with empowering affirmations that reinforce your ability to achieve your goals.

To further deepen your practice, consider setting aside dedicated time for visualization each day. Consistency is key to reinforcing your intentions and creating a strong energetic imprint in the universe. Whether it's in the morning to set the tone for your day or in the evening to reflect on your aspirations, establishing a routine will help you integrate visualization into your daily life.

As you progress in your visualization practice, you may also wish to explore the concept of vision boards. Vision boards are tangible representations of your goals and desires, created by compiling images, words, and symbols that resonate with your intentions. By visually surrounding yourself with representations of your aspirations, you reinforce your commitment to manifesting them. Place your vision board in a prominent location where you will see it regularly, allowing it to serve as a constant reminder of your goals and the energy you are directing toward them.

Another powerful technique for amplifying intentions is to engage in group visualization or intention-setting sessions. The collective energy generated by a group can significantly enhance the potency of your intentions. When individuals come together with a shared purpose, their combined energy creates a powerful resonance that amplifies the manifestation process. Consider joining or forming a group focused on intention-setting, meditation, or visualization. The support and encouragement of like-minded individuals can enhance your practice and foster a sense of community.

As you continue to refine your visualization skills, remember to remain open to the possibilities that arise. The universe may present opportunities and pathways to your goals that you had not anticipated. Trust in the process and remain flexible in your approach, allowing your intentions to unfold in ways that align with your highest good.

It's also essential to recognize that visualization is not a passive process; it requires active engagement and commitment. While visualization can create a powerful energetic imprint, it is equally important to take inspired action toward your goals. As you visualize your intentions, stay attuned to the signs and synchronicities that may guide you toward opportunities for growth and manifestation. Taking action reinforces your commitment to your goals and demonstrates your readiness to receive what you desire.

As you amplify your intentions through visualization, you will likely notice shifts in your energy and experiences. You may find that you attract opportunities, resources, and people who align with your goals. This phenomenon is often referred to as the Law of Attraction, which suggests that like attracts like. By raising your vibrational frequency through focused visualization, you create an energetic alignment that draws your desires closer to you.

12

Tuning into the Energy of Others: Empathetic Perception

"We are all connected, and every action we take has an impact on others."

Having immersed yourself in the alchemy of visualization to amplify your intentions, you now open the gateway to perceiving the subtle energies that others emit. This journey demands a heightened sensitivity, an attunement to the vibrational frequencies that resonate from every living being. To tune into these energies, you must first center yourself in a state of deep meditative stillness. Imagine that your consciousness is a perfectly tuned instrument, prepared to pick up the symphonic intricacies of the energy field of another person.

Begin by focusing on your breath, allowing it to create a rhythmic anchor that grounds you. As you breathe, extend your awareness

TUNING INTO THE ENERGY OF OTHERS: EMPATHETIC PERCEPTION

outward, envisioning it as an ethereal web that can touch and feel the energy of those around you. This practice of extending your awareness is akin to casting a net into the ocean of energy that surrounds you, enabling you to sense the currents and vibrations of others. When you encounter another's energy, don't just perceive it passively; engage with it. Use your mind's eye to visualize the colors, patterns, and textures that characterize this energy. Is it vibrant and dynamic, or perhaps subdued and fragmented? These observations will provide insight into the individual's emotional and mental state.

As you refine your perceptive abilities, you'll notice that the energy fields of others communicate a wealth of information. Every shift in their aura, every fluctuation in their vibrational frequency, speaks volumes about their inner world. Approach this practice with reverence and respect, understanding that you aren't merely an observer but a participant in a sacred exchange of energies. This exchange can deepen your connections and enhance your understanding of the emotional landscapes of those around you.

To effectively tune into the energy of others, it is essential to cultivate emotional intelligence. Emotional intelligence allows you to recognize, understand, and navigate your emotions while also attuning to the emotions of others. This skill enables you to become an empathetic listener, fostering deeper connections and enhancing your ability to read the energy of those around you. By developing emotional intelligence, you can create a safe space for others to express themselves, allowing their energy to flow freely and revealing their true essence.

A crucial aspect of tuning into the energy of others is to maintain a state of neutrality. When you approach someone with an open heart and mind, free from judgment or preconceived notions, you create an environment conducive to genuine connection. This neutrality allows you to perceive the energy of others without projecting your own fears or biases onto them. By remaining present and engaged, you can accurately sense their emotional state and respond with compassion and understanding.

To practice this, begin by engaging in conversations with individuals you feel comfortable with. As you listen to their words, pay attention to their body language, facial expressions, and overall energy. Notice how their energy shifts as they share their thoughts and feelings. Are they animated and excited, or do they appear withdrawn and heavy? By tuning into these subtle cues, you can gain valuable insights into their emotional state and respond in a way that fosters connection and support.

Another effective technique for tuning into the energy of others is to practice active listening. This involves fully engaging with the person speaking, allowing them to express themselves without interruption. As you listen, focus on their energy, allowing yourself to feel the vibrations of their words and emotions. This practice not only enhances your ability to read their energy but also strengthens your connection, as they feel heard and understood.

When tuning into the energy of others, it can be beneficial to practice grounding techniques. Grounding connects you to the Earth's energy, providing stability and strength as you navigate the emotional currents of those around you. To ground yourself, visualize roots extending from your feet into the Earth, anchoring you firmly in place. As you connect with the Earth's energy, imagine it rising up through your body, filling you with a sense of security and resilience. This grounding energy acts as a buffer against overwhelming emotions, allowing you

TUNING INTO THE ENERGY OF OTHERS: EMPATHETIC PERCEPTION

to maintain your energetic integrity while tuning into the energies of others.

Engaging with nature can also enhance your ability to sense and read energy fields. Nature presents a symphony of pure, unadulterated frequencies that can sharpen your perception. Spend time outdoors, allowing the natural world to replenish your energy and reinforce your connection to the universal field. Observe the subtle energies of plants, animals, and the environment around you. Each element of nature has its own unique vibrational frequency, and by attuning yourself to these energies, you can enhance your ability to read the energy of others.

As you continue to develop your skills in tuning into the energy of others, you may encounter situations that challenge your ability to maintain your energetic boundaries. It is crucial to recognize when you are absorbing the energy of others and to take steps to protect your own energy. This may involve setting clear boundaries, both energetically and emotionally, to ensure that you do not become overwhelmed by the energies of those around you.

One effective method for protecting your energy is to visualize a protective shield surrounding you. This shield can be imagined as a vibrant color that resonates with your energy. For example, you might choose a bright white light or a deep blue hue, depending on what feels most protective to you. As you visualize this shield, imagine it growing larger and more resilient with each breath you take. See it absorbing any negative energy that comes your way, transforming it into positive vibrations before it can penetrate your aura.

In addition to visualization, practicing self-care is essential for maintaining your energetic health. Engage in activities that replenish your energy and promote emotional well-being. This may include practices such as meditation, yoga, or spending time in nature. By prioritizing self-care, you create a strong foundation that allows you to tune into the energy of others without becoming depleted.

As you refine your ability to tune into the energy of others, you may begin to notice shifts in your perception and experience. You might find that you are more attuned to the subtle energies around you, able to sense the emotional states of others or the underlying currents of a situation. This heightened awareness allows you to navigate your interactions with greater ease and intention, fostering deeper connections and more harmonious relationships.

It is also important to remember that tuning into the energy of others is not solely about interpretation; it is also about connection. The more you engage with the energies around you, the more you will cultivate a sense of empathy and understanding for the experiences of others. This connection can foster deeper relationships and enhance your ability to support those around you.

As you continue on this journey of tuning into the energy of others, approach each experience with an open heart and mind. Embrace the mysteries that lie before you, for they are the doorways to a deeper understanding of yourself and the world around you. Trust in the process, and allow your intuition to guide you as you navigate the complexities of human energy dynamics.

13

Recognizing and Releasing Blockages: Clearing the Path to Spiritual Enlightenment

"Clear the clutter from your mind, and the path to enlightenment will become clear."

Often, the path to spiritual enlightenment is obstructed by unseen blockages that hinder the free flow of energy, demanding a keen awareness and deliberate effort to recognize and release these impediments. These blockages often reside in the subtle layers of your auric field, manifesting as energetic knots symbolic of unresolved emotional traumas, limiting beliefs, or subconscious fears. Recognizing these blockages requires a deep attunement to your inner vision—the clairvoyant eye—to perceive the disruptions in your energy matrix. This journey begins with a meditative state of heightened sensitivity, where you can scan your chakras and meridians, discerning areas of stagnation or disharmony.

To start this process, find a quiet space where you can sit comfortably without distractions. Close your eyes, and take a few deep, cleansing breaths. As you inhale, allow your body to relax, releasing any tension. Focus on your breath, letting it become rhythmic and steady. This grounding practice will help you center your awareness and prepare you for the exploration of your energy field.

As you settle into this meditative state, begin to visualize your chakras, the energy centers that govern your physical, emotional, and spiritual well-being. Scan each chakra, starting from the base of your spine and moving upward to the crown of your head. Pay attention to any sensations, tightness, or discomfort you may feel in these areas. Listen to your body's whispers, for it speaks through sensations, signaling the presence of energetic barriers. A tightness in your throat may indicate issues with communication, while discomfort in your solar plexus could point to unresolved emotional conflicts.

Recognizing these blockages is the first step toward releasing them. Once you have identified areas of stagnation, the next phase involves a multifaceted approach to releasing these impediments. This process blends symbolic interpretation with mystical elixirs, allowing you to engage with your energy on multiple levels.

Begin with the practice of intentional breathwork. Direct your breath to the area of stagnation, visualizing it as a radiant light imbued with healing frequencies. As you breathe in, imagine this light expanding and dissolving the knots of dense energy that have formed. With each exhale, visualize the release of this stagnant energy, allowing it to dissipate into the universe. This practice not only promotes physical relaxation but also facilitates emotional release, creating space for new, positive energy to flow.

Incorporating sound healing techniques can further enhance your ability to release blockages. Vibrational frequencies, such as those produced by singing bowls or tuning forks, resonate with your energy field, helping to dislodge stagnant energy. You might choose to listen to specific frequencies known for their healing properties, such as 528 Hz, which is often associated with transformation and miracles. As you immerse yourself in these sounds, allow the vibrations to penetrate your being, facilitating the release of any lingering blockages.

Additionally, engaging in energy cleansing rituals can be an effective way to purify your energetic field. Tools like sage, crystals, and sacred geometry patterns can act as conduits, amplifying your intention to release stagnant energy. Smudging with sage is a time-honored practice that involves burning sage and wafting the smoke around your body and space, allowing it to cleanse and purify your energy. As you perform this ritual, set a clear intention for what you wish to release, and visualize the smoke carrying away any negativity or blockages.

Crystals are another powerful ally in your journey of release. Specific crystals, such as black tourmaline, selenite, and amethyst, are known for their protective and purifying properties. You can hold these crystals during meditation or place them on the areas of your body where you feel blockages. As you do so, visualize the crystal's energy merging with your own, amplifying your intention to release and heal.

Sacred geometry can also play a significant role in your energy-clearing practices. Geometric patterns, such as the Flower of Life or the Metatron's Cube, represent the fundamental structures of the universe and can help align your energy with higher frequencies. You might choose to meditate on these shapes, visualizing them as part of your energetic landscape. As you focus on the patterns, imagine them dissolving any blockages and creating a harmonious flow of energy throughout your being.

Invoking the assistance of spiritual guides or ascended masters can further facilitate the release of deep-seated blockages. These higher beings can provide support and guidance as you navigate your healing journey. You might choose to call upon them during your meditation, requesting their intervention in releasing any energetic barriers that no longer serve you. Trust in their wisdom and guidance, and be open to the insights and messages that may arise during this process.

As you work through the process of recognizing and releasing blockages, it's essential to approach the practice with patience and compassion. Healing is not always linear, and it may take time to fully release deeply rooted energies. Be gentle with yourself as you navigate this journey, recognizing that each step you take brings you closer to greater clarity and freedom.

Regularly checking in with your energy field can help you maintain awareness of any new blockages that may arise. Consider incorporating a daily practice of self-reflection, where you take a few moments to assess your emotional and energetic state. This practice can involve journaling, meditation, or simply sitting in silence and tuning into your body. By cultivating this awareness, you can proactively address any blockages before they become entrenched.

In addition to personal practices, consider engaging in group healing sessions or workshops focused on energy work. These collective experiences can amplify your healing journey, as the energy of the group can create a powerful resonance that facilitates release and transformation. Sharing your experiences with others who are on a similar path can provide valuable insights and support as you navigate your journey of healing.

As you continue to recognize and release blockages, you may also wish to explore the concept of forgiveness. Holding onto past grievances or unresolved emotions can create significant energetic blockages. Practicing forgiveness—both toward yourself and others—can free you from the weight of these burdens. This process may involve journaling about your feelings, engaging in guided meditations focused on forgiveness, or having open conversations with those involved.

Forgiveness is not about condoning past actions; it is about liberating yourself from the emotional ties that bind you to those experiences. By releasing these ties, you create space for new energy to flow into your life, allowing for healing and growth.

Another powerful tool for recognizing and releasing blockages is the practice of visualization. As you meditate, visualize any blockages as physical objects within your body or energy field. Imagine these objects taking on specific shapes, colors, or textures. Once you have identified them, visualize yourself gently dissolving or removing these blockages. You might imagine them melting away, disintegrating into light, or being transformed into something positive. This process can create a profound sense of release and liberation.

As you progress on your journey of recognizing and releasing blockages, remember that you are not alone. Many individuals face similar challenges on their path to healing and self-discovery. Seeking support from friends, family, or professional practitioners can provide valuable insights and encouragement. Whether through therapy, energy healing sessions, or community support groups, connecting with others can foster a sense of belonging and understanding.

14

Mastering the Art of Energetic Projection: Shaping Reality with Intention

"The power of thought is limitless. Use it wisely."

With the purification of your energetic field, you can now harness and project your refined energy, mastering the art of energetic projection to influence and manifest within the subtle domains. This process begins with cultivating an acute awareness of your energy body, perceiving its vibrations and resonances as a symphony of frequencies. Visualize your energy as a radiant light capable of extending beyond the confines of your physical form, intertwining with the universal energy matrix.

To effectively project your energy, you must first ground yourself. Envision roots extending from your being into the Earth's core, drawing stability and strength. This foundation is essential, as it allows you to channel your energy through your chakras, particularly focusing on the third eye and crown chakras, which serve as conduits for higher frequencies. These energy centers are crucial for accessing the subtle realms and amplifying your energetic projection.

Once you have established your grounding, engage in meditative practices that elevate your vibrational state. Utilize breathwork to synchronize your energy flow, inhaling deeply to draw in cosmic energy and exhaling to release any residual stagnation. As your vibrational frequency ascends, imagine your energy field expanding, reaching out to touch and influence the energetic fabric around you. This visualization is key; it allows you to perceive the interconnectedness of all beings and the potential impact of your energy projection.

Symbolically, understand that energetic projection is akin to casting a net into the ocean of existence. Your intentions, imbued with clarity and purpose, are the threads of this net. Through focused visualization, project these intentions into the ether, allowing them to ripple through the quantum field, catalyzing transformation and manifestation. This process is not merely about sending out energy; it is about creating a harmonious resonance that aligns with your desires and aspirations.

To deepen your practice, begin by setting clear intentions for your energetic projection. What do you wish to manifest? Is it healing for yourself or others, abundance, love, or perhaps clarity in a specific situation? Write down your intentions, articulating them in positive, present-tense language. For example, instead of saying, "I want to be healthy," rephrase it to "I am vibrant and full of health." This subtle shift in language reinforces the belief that your intention is already a reality, enhancing the potency of your projection.

Once your intentions are clear, return to your meditative state. Focus on your breath, allowing it to guide you into a deeper state of relaxation.

As you breathe, visualize your intentions as radiant light, pulsating with energy. See this light expanding from your heart center, flowing through your chakras, and radiating outward into the universe. Imagine it intertwining with the energy of others, creating a web of connection that amplifies your intentions.

Engaging in visualization techniques can further enhance your ability to project energy. Picture your intentions as vibrant colors or symbols, each representing a specific aspect of what you wish to manifest. For instance, if your intention is to cultivate love, visualize a warm, pink light enveloping you and extending outward, touching the hearts of those around you. This imagery not only reinforces your intention but also creates a powerful energetic resonance that can influence others.

As you practice energetic projection, it is essential to remain open to receiving feedback from the universe. Pay attention to the signs and synchronicities that may arise in your life. These can serve as indicators that your energy is being received and that your intentions are taking root. Trust in the process and remain patient, as energetic projection is not always instantaneous. It often requires time for the energy to shift and manifest in the physical realm.

In addition to visualization and intention-setting, consider incorporating sound into your energetic projection practice. Sound is a powerful medium for transmitting energy and can enhance your ability to project your intentions. You might choose to chant mantras, use singing bowls, or listen to specific frequencies that resonate with your goals. The vibrations created by sound can help to amplify your energy, creating a more profound impact on the energetic field.

Another effective technique for mastering energetic projection is to practice with a partner or in a group setting. When individuals come together with a shared purpose, their collective energy can create a powerful resonance that amplifies each person's intentions. Consider organizing a group meditation or intention-setting session, where participants can project their energy together. This collaborative approach fosters a sense of community and enhances the potency of your projections.

As you continue to refine your skills in energetic projection, it is important to maintain a strong connection to your own energy. Regular self-care practices, such as grounding, meditation, and energy cleansing, will help you stay attuned to your energetic state. By nurturing your own energy, you create a solid foundation for effective projection, allowing you to influence the energies around you with clarity and purpose.

In the journey of mastering energetic projection, you may encounter challenges or obstacles. It is essential to approach these experiences with curiosity and openness. If you find that your energy feels stagnant or blocked, take time to reflect on any underlying emotions or beliefs that may be hindering your ability to project effectively. Engaging in practices that promote emotional release, such as journaling or energy healing, can help you clear these blockages and restore the flow of energy.

Additionally, consider exploring the concept of energetic boundaries. As you project your energy into the world, it is crucial to maintain a sense of personal integrity and protection. Visualize a protective shield surrounding you, ensuring that you remain grounded and centered as you extend your energy outward. This shield can be imagined as a vibrant color that resonates with your energy, creating a barrier against any negative influences or unwanted energies.

15

Protecting Your Energy From Draining: Forging Your Energetic Fortress

"The energy you attract is a reflection of the energy you project."

To safeguard your energy from draining, envision a luminous shield enveloping your aura—a sacred barrier forged through intention and fortified by your unwavering will. This radiant cocoon, shimmering with iridescent hues, serves as your personal sanctuary against external energetic assaults. By harnessing the esoteric principles of energetic alchemy, you can transmute potential threats into neutral or even beneficial frequencies.

Begin by grounding yourself, connecting with the Earth's primordial essence. Visualize roots extending from your feet into the core of Gaia, drawing up nourishing vitality. Simultaneously, focus on your breath—the prana that interlaces your being with the cosmos. With each inhalation, draw in universal energy; with each exhalation, expel any residual negativity.

Invoke the sacred geometry of the toroidal field, a self-sustaining flow of energy that circulates through your chakras and auric layers. Imagine this torus as a dynamic, pulsating shield, its movement analogous to the perpetual dance of the cosmos. This cyclical motion not only deflects harmful vibrations but also perpetuates your energetic sovereignty.

Employ mantras or affirmations imbued with metaphysical significance. Recite phrases such as "I am sovereign," "I am protected," and "I am whole," infusing each syllable with intent. Words charged with vibrational potency act as catalysts, solidifying your energetic defense.

As you progress in your practice, you will find that maintaining this energetic shield requires consistent effort and awareness. It is essential to cultivate a mindset that prioritizes your energy and recognizes the importance of setting boundaries. This act of self-love not only protects you but also empowers you to create healthier relationships and a more positive environment.

To further enhance your energetic protection, consider incorporating daily rituals into your routine. These can include meditation, visualization exercises, or even simple practices like taking a moment to breathe deeply and center yourself throughout the day.

In moments of stress or overwhelm, remember to return to your breath. Breathe in deeply, allowing the nourishing energy of the Earth to fill your being, and exhale any tension or negativity you may be holding onto. This practice not only grounds you but also reinforces the protective shield surrounding your aura.

Additionally, be mindful of the energies you allow into your space. Surround yourself with individuals who uplift and inspire you, and be discerning about the influences you engage with. Whether it's social media, news, or even conversations, the energy of these interactions can significantly impact your own energetic state.

Creating a protective bubble around yourself can be a powerful visualization tool. Picture a soft, white light surrounding you, acting as a barrier against negativity. Whenever you feel your energy being drained, return to this visualization and reinforce the shield with your intention.

Incorporating crystals into your energetic practice can also be beneficial. Certain stones, such as black tourmaline, selenite, and amethyst, are known for their protective properties. Carry them with you or place them in your environment to help absorb negative energies and enhance your energetic shield.

As you deepen your understanding of energetic protection, consider exploring the concept of energetic hygiene. This practice involves regularly cleansing your energy field and environment to prevent the buildup of unwanted energies. Techniques such as smudging with sage, using sound healing, or taking salt baths can effectively clear your energetic space.

It's also important to recognize the signs of energy depletion. Symptoms such as fatigue, irritability, or a sense of being overwhelmed can indicate that your energetic boundaries have been compromised. When you notice these signs, take immediate action to restore your energy. This might involve retreating to a quiet space, engaging in self-care practices, or reconnecting with nature.

Establishing clear boundaries is vital in protecting your energy. Learn to say no when necessary and prioritize your well-being over the expectations of others. This can be challenging, especially for those who are empathetic or sensitive to the needs of others, but it is a crucial aspect of maintaining your energetic sovereignty.

In addition to setting boundaries, cultivate a practice of self-reflection. Regularly assess your emotional and energetic state, and be honest with yourself about what drains your energy and what replenishes it. This awareness will empower you to make conscious choices that support your energetic health.

As you navigate your daily life, remember that you have the power to protect your energy. Each moment presents an opportunity to reinforce your shield and maintain your sovereignty. By remaining intentional and aware, you can create an environment that nurtures your spirit and uplifts your energy.

Engaging with the principles of energetic alchemy allows you to transform challenges into opportunities for growth. When faced with negativity or draining situations, practice reframing your perspective. Ask yourself how you can learn from the experience or what positive aspects you can extract from it.

Incorporating mindfulness into your daily routine can also enhance your ability to protect your energy. Mindfulness encourages you to be present in each moment, allowing you to notice when your energy is being affected by external influences. This heightened awareness enables you to take proactive steps to safeguard your energy before it becomes depleted.

16

Navigating the Multidimensional Realms : Lattice Of Existence

"The universe is not only stranger than we imagine; it is stranger than we can imagine."

As you venture into your journey through the multi-dimensional domains, envision yourself traversing the intricate lattice of existence where each layer reveals hidden truths and cosmic wisdom. Imagine the ethereal threads that interlace these realms, each a conduit of esoteric energy resonating at frequencies beyond the mundane. Your consciousness, now attuned to these vibrations, acts as a celestial navigator, guiding you through the labyrinth of dimensions.

Begin by anchoring your awareness in the present moment, grounding yourself in the tangible reality before ascending into higher planes. This grounding is crucial, as it provides you with a stable foundation from which to explore the vastness of existence. As you transcend into these higher realms, visualize the astral gateways; each portal symbolizes existential milestones that mark your spiritual journey. These thresholds are often guarded by archetypal entities, embodying profound knowledge and spiritual guardianship. Engaging with these entities through symbolic interpretation allows you to decipher their messages, which serve as keys to revealing deeper layers of the cosmic tapestry.

In these dimensions, time and space become fluid, non-linear constructs. You must embrace this fluidity, allowing your intuitive faculties to perceive the interwoven patterns of existence. This perception is essential, as it enables you to recognize the synchronicities and connections that permeate all levels of reality. Focus on the harmonic convergence of energy frequencies—the symphony of vibrations that orchestrate the cosmic dance. By harmonizing your inner energy field with these frequencies, you can access dimensions teeming with arcane wisdom and transformative power.

To navigate these multi-dimensional realms effectively, it is essential to cultivate a heightened state of awareness. This awareness allows you to perceive subtle shifts in energy and to recognize when you are being called to explore new dimensions. Techniques such as meditation, breathwork, and visualization can help you attune your consciousness to these higher frequencies. Regular practice of these techniques will enhance your ability to access and engage with the multi-dimensional aspects of your being.

As you embark on this journey, you may encounter various archetypal figures that represent different aspects of your psyche and spiritual evolution. These figures can serve as guides, mentors, or even reflections of your own inner challenges. Engaging with them through meditation or dream work can provide valuable insights into your personal growth and the lessons you are meant to learn in this lifetime.

In addition to archetypal figures, you may also encounter spiritual guardians that protect and guide you through these realms. These guardians can take many forms, from mythological beings to animal spirits, and their presence can offer reassurance and support as you navigate the complexities of multi-dimensional existence. Establishing a relationship with these guardians can deepen your understanding of your spiritual path and enhance your ability to traverse the various layers of reality.

As you explore these dimensions, remember that your thoughts and intentions play a crucial role in shaping your experiences. The vibrational frequency of your thoughts can either elevate or hinder your journey. Therefore, it is essential to cultivate a mindset of positivity, curiosity, and openness. By maintaining a high vibrational state, you can attract experiences and insights that align with your highest good.

One of the most profound aspects of navigating multi-dimensional realms is the realization that all dimensions exist simultaneously. This understanding allows you to access the wisdom and experiences of your other selves across various timelines and realities. By tapping into these alternate versions of yourself, you can gain insights that inform your current life and facilitate healing on multiple levels. This process is akin to updating the software of your consciousness, where improvements in one area can lead to enhancements throughout your entire being.

Engaging with the concept of bi-location can also enhance your ability to navigate these realms. Bi-location refers to the practice of consciously existing in two places at once, allowing you to experience different dimensions simultaneously. This practice requires a deep level of focus and intention, as well as a willingness to surrender to the flow of energy. By mastering bi-location, you can access the wisdom and insights of other dimensions while remaining anchored in your current reality.

In your exploration of multi-dimensional realms, consider the importance of integrating your experiences into your daily life. This integration process is essential for grounding the insights and wisdom you gain during your journeys. Take time to reflect on your experiences, journal your insights, and share your discoveries with others. This practice not only reinforces your understanding but also contributes to the collective consciousness of humanity.

It is also essential to establish a personal haven within these multi-dimensional spaces. Creating a spiritual anchor point allows you to return to a place of safety and comfort whenever you feel overwhelmed or disoriented. This haven can be a visualization of a serene landscape, a sacred space within your mind, or even a physical location that resonates with your soul. By returning to this haven, you can recharge your energy and gain clarity before continuing your exploration.

As you delve deeper into the multi-dimensional realms, you may encounter challenges that test your resolve and commitment to your spiritual path. These challenges can manifest as fears, doubts, or obstacles that seem insurmountable. However, it is essential to recognize these challenges as opportunities for growth and transformation. Embrace them with an open heart and a willingness to learn, for they often hold the key to unlocking deeper levels of understanding.

In moments of uncertainty, trust in your intuition and inner guidance. Your higher self is always present, offering support and wisdom as you navigate the complexities of multi-dimensional existence. By cultivating a strong connection with your higher self, you can access the insights and guidance needed to overcome challenges and continue your journey with confidence.

Remember that your journey is unique and deeply personal. Each individual's experience of multi-dimensionality will differ based on their beliefs, intentions, and spiritual practices. Embrace your individuality and honor your unique path, for it is through this authenticity that you will uncover the most profound truths about yourself and the universe.

17

The Role Of Breathwork In Energy Control : The Bridge Of Consciousness

"The breath is the bridge which connects life to consciousness, which unites your body to your thoughts."

Harnessing the primal force of breath grants access to mastering your energetic essence, harmonizing the currents of your inner universe with the pulsating rhythms of the cosmos. Breath work, the sacred art of consciously controlling your inhalations and exhalations, serves as a conduit to channel pranic energy—the life force that permeates all existence. Each deliberate breath becomes a symphony, a rhythmic dance that fine-tunes your vibrational frequency, attuning your physical and ethereal bodies to higher states of awareness.

When you engage in pranayama or other breath work techniques, you are not merely oxygenating your blood; you are invoking an ancient alchemy that transmutes mundane energies into divine consciousness. Through methods such as Nadi Shodhana (alternate nostril breathing), you purify the subtle channels or nadis, ensuring the free flow of energy and dissolving blockages that impede spiritual ascension. This purification process is akin to clearing the fog from a mirror, allowing the luminous reflection of your true self to shine through.

Breath work serves as a potent tool for grounding and centering, anchoring your energetic field within the Earth's magnetic grid while simultaneously connecting you to celestial domains. The act of conscious breathing integrates the microcosm of your being with the macrocosm of the universe, creating a harmonious resonance that amplifies your energetic influence. Each breath is not just a physical act; it is a metaphysical invocation, a sacred whisper to the universe commanding the alignment of your energetic frequencies with the cosmic symphony.

To begin your journey into the transformative practice of breath work, it is essential to establish a foundational understanding of its principles. The breath is a vital force that sustains life, yet many individuals fail to utilize it to its fullest potential. In our fast-paced world, shallow and irregular breathing patterns have become the norm, leading to increased stress, anxiety, and disconnection from our true selves. By consciously engaging with your breath, you can reclaim this vital energy and harness it for personal empowerment and spiritual growth.

Start by cultivating awareness of your breath. Find a quiet space where you can sit comfortably, close your eyes, and turn your attention inward. Begin to observe the natural rhythm of your breath without attempting to change it. Notice the sensations in your body as you inhale and exhale, allowing yourself to become fully present in the moment. This practice of mindful breathing serves as a gateway to deeper states of consciousness and prepares you for more advanced breath work techniques.

Once you have established a sense of awareness, you can explore various breath work techniques that resonate with your energy and intentions. One powerful method is diaphragmatic breathing, also known as abdominal breathing. This technique encourages deeper inhalations that fill the lungs completely, allowing for optimal oxygen exchange and relaxation. To practice diaphragmatic breathing, place one hand on your chest and the other on your abdomen. Inhale deeply through your nose, allowing your abdomen to rise while keeping your chest relatively still. Exhale slowly through your mouth, feeling your abdomen fall. Repeat this process for several minutes, focusing on the rise and fall of your abdomen as you breathe.

Another effective technique is the "4-7-8" breath, which can be particularly beneficial for calming the mind and reducing stress. To practice this technique, inhale deeply through your nose for a count of four, hold your breath for a count of seven, and exhale slowly through your mouth for a count of eight. This rhythmic pattern helps to regulate your breath and promotes a sense of tranquility, making it an excellent tool for grounding and centering.

As you become more comfortable with these foundational techniques, you can explore more advanced breath work practices such as Nadi Shodhana or alternate nostril breathing. This technique involves closing one nostril while inhaling through the other, then switching nostrils to exhale. This practice balances the energies within the body, harmonizing the left and right hemispheres of the brain and promoting a sense of calm and clarity.

To perform Nadi Shodhana, sit comfortably with your spine straight.

Use your right thumb to close your right nostril and inhale deeply through your left nostril. Close your left nostril with your right ring finger, release your right nostril, and exhale through it. Inhale through the right nostril, close it, and exhale through the left. Continue this pattern for several rounds, focusing on the flow of energy and the balance it creates within your being.

As you delve deeper into breath work, you will discover that your breath can also serve as a powerful tool for emotional release and healing. Many individuals carry emotional baggage that manifests as tension or stagnation in the body. By consciously engaging with your breath, you can facilitate the release of these trapped emotions and restore balance to your energetic field.

One effective technique for emotional release is the "Breath of Fire," a rapid and rhythmic breathing pattern that energizes the body and clears mental fog. To practice this technique, sit comfortably with your spine straight. Inhale deeply through your nose, then exhale forcefully through your nose while contracting your abdominal muscles. Focus on the exhalation, allowing the inhalation to occur passively. Continue this rapid breathing for one to two minutes, then return to normal breathing and observe the sensations in your body.

In addition to its physical and emotional benefits, breath work also enhances spiritual connection and awareness. As you engage in conscious breathing, you open yourself to higher states of consciousness and the wisdom of the universe. This connection can lead to profound insights, intuitive guidance, and a deeper understanding of your purpose and path.

To further enhance your spiritual practice, consider incorporating visualization techniques into your breath work. As you breathe deeply, visualize a beam of light shining down from the cosmos, entering through the crown of your head and filling your entire being with radiant energy. With each inhalation, imagine this light cleansing and energizing you, and with each exhalation, release any unwanted energy, stress, or negativity you may be holding. This visualization amplifies the effects of your breath work, allowing you to connect with the divine and access higher realms of consciousness.

As you explore the mystical practice of breath work, it is essential to integrate these techniques into your daily life. Consistency is key to experiencing the full benefits of breath work, so consider setting aside dedicated time each day for your practice. Whether you choose to engage in a formal session or simply take a few moments throughout the day to focus on your breath, the act of conscious breathing will enhance your overall well-being and energetic control.

Incorporating breath work into your daily routine can also help you navigate the challenges of modern life with greater ease and resilience. When faced with stress, anxiety, or overwhelm, returning to your breath can provide a powerful anchor, grounding you in the present moment and allowing you to respond with clarity and composure.

As you continue to deepen your practice, you may find that breath work opens doors to new dimensions of awareness and understanding. The breath serves as a bridge between the physical and spiritual realms, allowing you to access the wisdom and guidance of your higher self. By cultivating a strong connection with your breath, you empower yourself to navigate the complexities of existence with grace and confidence.

18

Activating the Third Eye and Crown: A Journey Towards Enlightenment

"The mind is everything. What you think you become."

With your breath now a bridge between dimensions, you awaken the latent power of the third eye and crown, gateways to higher planes of consciousness and divine wisdom. These chakras, the Ajna and Sahasrara, are not merely vortices of energy; they are sacred conduits to the omniscient dimensions. As you explore deeper into their activation, you will begin perceiving the subtle symphony of the cosmos—an intricate dance of frequencies shaping your reality.

Start with the third eye, situated between your brows. Visualize an indigo lotus unfurling its petals, each one resonating with ancient esoteric truths. Focus your intention on this locus, allowing a pulsating energy to permeate your consciousness. Feel the vibrational shift as your pineal gland, the physical counterpart, begins to hum with cosmic resonance. This is the seat of inner vision, where intuition sharpens and the veils of illusion thin.

To activate the third eye, begin with breath work, as it plays a crucial role in this process. Engage in deep, conscious breathing, inhaling through your nose and exhaling through your mouth. With each breath, visualize energy flowing into your third eye, awakening its potential. As you breathe in, imagine drawing in divine light, and as you exhale, release any blockages or negativity that may hinder your perception. This practice not only oxygenates your body but also aligns your energetic frequencies with the higher vibrations of the universe.

As you continue to focus on your third eye, you may want to incorporate specific techniques to enhance its activation. One effective method is Nadi Shodhana, or alternate nostril breathing. This technique balances the energies within your body, harmonizing the left and right hemispheres of your brain. To practice, sit comfortably and use your right thumb to close your right nostril. Inhale deeply through your left nostril, then close it with your right ring finger. Open your right nostril and exhale through it. Inhale through the right nostril, close it, and exhale through the left. Repeat this cycle for several rounds, focusing on the flow of energy and the balance it creates.

In addition to breath work, consider incorporating meditation into your practice. Find a quiet space where you can sit comfortably and close your eyes. Begin by focusing on your breath, allowing it to become slow and steady. Once you feel centered, bring your attention to your third eye. Visualize the indigo lotus expanding and contracting with each breath, becoming more vibrant and alive. As you meditate, invite insights and intuitive guidance to emerge, trusting that your third eye is opening to the wisdom of the universe.

Now elevate your awareness to the crown chakra, poised at the apex of your head. Picture a thousand-petaled lotus, radiant and pure, channeling divine light into your being. As this light cascades through you, it purifies your energy field, linking you to the universal mind. The activation of the Sahasrara transcends personal insight, facilitating a union with the infinite—a state known as Samadhi. In this state, you experience a profound sense of interconnectedness with all that is, feeling the pulse of the cosmos within you.

To activate the crown chakra, continue your breath work, allowing the energy to flow from your third eye to your crown. Visualize the divine light from the lotus at your crown expanding outward, enveloping your entire being in a cocoon of radiant energy. As you breathe in, feel this light entering through your crown, filling you with pure consciousness. As you exhale, release any limiting beliefs or attachments that may obstruct your connection to the divine.

Incorporating sound into your practice can also enhance the activation of your third eye and crown chakras. Chanting mantras, such as "Om," resonates with the frequencies of these chakras, creating vibrations that facilitate their opening. Find a comfortable position, close your eyes, and begin to chant the mantra, allowing the sound to resonate through your body. Feel the vibrations stimulating your third eye and crown, amplifying your connection to higher consciousness.

As you explore further into the mystical practice of activating your third eye and crown, remember that patience and consistency are essential. The journey toward enlightenment is a sacred pilgrimage, and each step brings you closer to your true self. Establish a daily practice that includes breath work, meditation, and sound, allowing these techniques to become integral parts of your spiritual routine.

In addition to these practices, consider incorporating yoga into your journey. Certain poses, such as Child's Pose and Downward-Facing Dog, can help stimulate the third eye and crown chakras. While in Child's Pose, rest your forehead on the ground, allowing the energy to flow into your third eye. In Downward-Facing Dog, let your head hang, encouraging blood flow to your brain and enhancing your connection to your higher self.

As you deepen your practice, you may also want to explore the use of crystals to support the activation of your third eye and crown chakras. Crystals such as amethyst, lapis lazuli, and clear quartz are known for their metaphysical properties that enhance intuition and spiritual connection. Hold these crystals during meditation or place them on your third eye and crown while lying down, allowing their energy to amplify your own.

Throughout this journey, trust in the process. The activation of the third eye and crown is not a destination but a continuous unfolding of your consciousness. As you cultivate your practice, you may find that your mental faculties are enhanced, spiritual insights are amplified, and a profound sense of interconnectedness with the cosmos emerges.

Engage with your intuition, allowing it to guide you in your practice. Pay attention to the subtle shifts in your energy and awareness as you activate these chakras. You may experience vivid dreams, heightened sensitivity to energy, or a deeper understanding of your purpose. Embrace these experiences as signs of your awakening, and allow them to inform your journey.

As you navigate this sacred path, remember that the journey of activating the third eye and crown is a deeply personal one. Each individual's experience will differ based on their unique energy and spiritual background. Honor your intuition and inner guidance, allowing them to lead you toward the practices and techniques that resonate most with you.

In moments of doubt or uncertainty, return to your breath. Breathe deeply, anchoring yourself in the present moment. Trust that you are exactly where you need to be on your journey, and that the universe is supporting your growth and evolution.

As you continue to activate your third eye and crown, you may find that your perception of reality begins to shift. The subtle symphony of the cosmos will become more apparent, revealing the interconnectedness of all things. You will learn to see beyond the physical realm, accessing the wisdom of the universe and tapping into the divine consciousness that flows through you.

19

Deciphering Symbols and Energy Codes

"Symbols are the language of the soul."

Delving into the domain of symbols and energy codes, you set out on a journey to decipher the mystical lexicon that bridges the mundane with the metaphysical. This endeavor requires you to attune your consciousness to the subtle frequencies that energize these symbols, transforming abstract imagery into profound understanding. Symbols are not mere decorations; they are powerful conduits of energy and meaning, each carrying its unique vibration and wisdom.

Begin by immersing yourself in the study of archetypal symbols—those universal motifs that resonate through the collective unconscious. Symbols like the ankh, the Flower of Life, or the Ouroboros encapsulate complex energy signatures that can unlock deeper layers of your understanding. The ankh, for instance, is an ancient Egyptian symbol representing eternal life and the interconnectedness of all existence. It serves as a reminder of the cyclical nature of life and death, reflecting the continuous flow of energy that permeates our reality.

As you engage with these symbols, visualize them pulsing with life, their energy fields intertwining with your own aura. Imagine the ankh glowing with vibrant energy, transmitting ancient wisdom and revealing latent psychic faculties within you. Allow the intricate patterns of these symbols to permeate your awareness, enhancing your perception and understanding of the energies at play in your life.

Energy codes often embedded within sacred geometries or esoteric scripts serve as the language of the cosmos. By deciphering these codes, you access the vibrational blueprint of reality itself. Sacred geometry, such as the Flower of Life, is not only visually stunning but also represents the fundamental patterns of creation. Each overlapping circle in the Flower of Life symbolizes the interconnectedness of all living beings, reflecting the divine order that governs the universe.

To deepen your connection with these energy codes, utilize tools such as the pendulum or dowsing rods. These instruments can help you interact with the subtle frequencies of the symbols, translating the ethereal into the tangible. The pendulum, for example, acts as a bridge between your conscious mind and the intuitive wisdom of your higher self. By asking specific questions and observing the pendulum's movements, you can gain insights into the meanings and energies associated with various symbols.

Dowsing rods, traditionally made from Y-shaped branches or L-shaped metal rods, can also be effective in detecting energy fields and accessing information from the collective unconscious. When you walk with the rods, they may respond to the presence of energy, guiding you to areas of significance or revealing hidden truths. This practice requires you to be centered and focused, allowing your subconscious mind to influence the movement of the rods as you seek answers.

Trust in your intuitive faculties as they reveal the layers of meaning concealed within each symbol. Your inner vision is paramount in this process, allowing you to perceive the subtle energies that accompany these symbols. As you engage with them, you may notice shifts in your energy field, heightened awareness, or even psychic insights. Keep a metaphysical journal to document your experiences, recording not only the symbols and codes you encounter but also the shifts in your consciousness.

This practice of journaling creates a personal codex of mystical insights—a roadmap guiding you through the labyrinthine corridors of esoteric knowledge. Reflect on your experiences, noting any themes or patterns that emerge. Over time, you may find that certain symbols resonate more deeply with you, revealing their significance in your spiritual journey. This codex becomes a valuable resource, helping you track your progress and deepen your understanding of the symbols and energy codes that shape your reality.

As you master the art of deciphering symbols and energy codes, you lay the groundwork for deeper explorations into the mysteries of the universe. Each symbol you encounter serves as a key, unlocking new realms of understanding and facilitating your alchemical journey of transforming energy patterns. The process of deciphering these symbols is akin to peeling back layers of an onion, revealing deeper truths and insights with each layer you remove.

Engaging with symbols also invites you to explore the relationship between the microcosm and macrocosm. The symbols you encounter in your personal journey are reflections of universal truths, resonating with the collective consciousness of humanity. As you deepen your understanding of these symbols, you may find that they resonate with the experiences of others, creating a sense of connection and unity.

Consider the Yin and Yang symbol, which represents the balance of opposing forces in the universe. This symbol serves as a reminder that light and dark, masculine and feminine, and other dualities exist in harmony, contributing to the overall balance of existence. By understanding the interplay of these forces within yourself, you can cultivate a greater sense of equilibrium in your life.

Another powerful symbol to explore is the Tree of Life, which appears in various cultures and spiritual traditions. This symbol represents the interconnectedness of all living beings and the cycles of life, death, and rebirth. By meditating on the Tree of Life, you can tap into its energy, fostering a sense of grounding and connection to the earth while also reaching for the higher realms of consciousness.

As you continue your journey of deciphering symbols and energy codes, remain open to the insights and revelations that arise. Each symbol holds a unique frequency and message, inviting you to explore its depths. Allow your intuition to guide you as you engage with these symbols, trusting that they will reveal their meanings in divine timing.

Incorporating rituals into your practice can also enhance your connection to symbols and energy codes. Create a sacred space where you can meditate on the symbols that resonate with you. Light candles, burn incense, or play soft music to create an atmosphere conducive to exploration. As you engage with the symbols, visualize their energy enveloping you, infusing your being with their wisdom.

Consider performing a ritual where you choose a symbol that resonates with you and create a physical representation of it. This could be through drawing, painting, or crafting an object that embodies the symbol's energy. As you create, focus on the intention behind the symbol and how it relates to your life. This act of creation can deepen your connection to the symbol and enhance your understanding of its significance.

As you cultivate your practice, you may find that your ability to perceive symbols and energy codes expands. You may begin to notice symbols appearing in your dreams, everyday life, or even in nature. These synchronicities serve as reminders of the interconnectedness of all things and the guidance available to you from the universe.

Engaging with symbols also invites you to explore the concept of light codes—energetic imprints embedded within the light itself. These codes carry information from higher dimensions and can activate your consciousness, accelerating your spiritual growth. By attuning yourself to these light codes, you can unlock transformative potential and deepen your understanding of the universe.

To access light codes, create a meditative practice where you focus on the light surrounding you. Visualize it as a vibrant, pulsating energy that holds the keys to higher states of awareness. As you breathe deeply, invite the light codes to enter your being, allowing them to activate dormant aspects of your consciousness. Trust that the insights and wisdom contained within these codes will unfold in alignment with your spiritual journey.

20

Transmuting Negative Energy Patterns

"The only way to deal with the negative is to turn it into a positive."

Having attuned your consciousness to the subtle vibrational frequencies of symbols and energy codes, you now navigate the intricate process of transmuting negative energy patterns—an alchemical practice that transforms discordant vibrations into harmonious resonance. This sacred act demands an acute awareness of the energetic imprints that permeate your aura, necessitating a profound understanding of the interplay between intention and manifestation.

Begin by centering yourself in a state of meditative awareness, allowing your inner vision to perceive the energetic disturbances within your field. Imagine these patterns as swirling vortices of shadow within the luminous matrix of your etheric field. These shadows represent the negative energy patterns that have accumulated over time, often as a result of emotional trauma, environmental influences, or limiting beliefs. By visualizing these disturbances, you create the space necessary for transformation.

Invoke the transmutative power of the violet flame, an esoteric symbol of purification and transformation. This flame, often associated with Saint Germain, is known for its ability to transmute negative energies into positive ones. Through both visualization and incantation, envision the violet flame enveloping the negative energy within you. Picture its transformative essence dissolving the discord and reinstating equilibrium in your energetic field. As you visualize this process, repeat affirmations such as, "I am the violet flame, transforming all negativity into light," allowing the words to resonate deeply within your being.

Next, focus on your breath. Each inhalation draws in divine prana, charged with frequencies of love and harmony, while each exhalation expels residual negativity. This cyclical breath work acts as a conduit for energy purification, reinforcing the alchemical process. As you breathe in, visualize the divine energy filling your body, illuminating the shadows and dispelling them with each exhalation. This practice not only purifies your energy field but also enhances your overall well-being, promoting a sense of calm and clarity.

To further assist in transmutation, employ sacred geometry. Visualize the Flower of Life or the Merkabah star integrating these symbols within your energy field. The Flower of Life, composed of multiple overlapping circles, represents the interconnectedness of all life and the sacred patterns that govern the universe. Its geometric perfection serves to recalibrate and realign disrupted frequencies, elevating the vibrational quality of your auric space. As you visualize these sacred shapes, feel their energy harmonizing with your own, creating a protective barrier that shields you from negative influences.

The Merkabah, or the chariot of light, is another powerful symbol for energy transmutation. It is often depicted as a star tetrahedron, representing the union of the physical and spiritual realms. By visualizing the Merkabah around you, you create a dynamic energy field that facilitates the movement of energy, allowing for the release of negativity and the influx of positive vibrations. Imagine the Merkabah spinning around you, creating a vortex that draws in light and expels darkness.

As you engage in these practices, it is essential to cultivate an acute awareness of your thoughts and emotions. Negative energy patterns often stem from unresolved feelings or limiting beliefs that reside within your subconscious. By bringing these issues to the surface, you can begin to address and release them. Journaling can be a valuable tool in this process. Write down any negative thoughts or emotions that arise, along with the circumstances surrounding them. This practice not only provides clarity but also serves as a means of releasing pent-up energy.

In addition to journaling, consider incorporating movement into your transmutation practice. Physical activity, such as yoga or dance, can help release stagnant energy and promote a sense of flow within your body. As you move, visualize the negative energy being expelled from your body, replaced by vibrant, healing light. This dynamic expression allows you to connect with your physical self while facilitating the energetic shift needed for transformation.

Another powerful technique for transmuting negative energy patterns is the use of sound. Sound vibrations can penetrate the energetic layers of your being, breaking up stagnant energy and promoting healing. Consider using singing bowls, tuning forks, or even your own voice to create sound frequencies that resonate with your intention for transformation. As you produce sound, visualize the vibrations traveling through your body, dissolving negativity and inviting in harmony.

In moments of heightened emotional distress, grounding techniques can also be beneficial. Grounding connects you to the Earth's energy, providing stability and support during times of upheaval. Stand barefoot on the ground, focusing on the sensations in your feet as they connect with the earth. Visualize roots extending from your feet into the ground, anchoring you firmly while drawing up the nurturing energy of the Earth. This practice helps to balance your energy and restore a sense of calm amidst chaos.

As you continue to explore the transmutation of negative energy patterns, remember that this process is not linear. It requires patience and compassion for yourself as you navigate the complexities of your emotions and experiences. There may be moments when you feel overwhelmed or uncertain; these feelings are part of the journey. Embrace them as opportunities for growth and transformation.

To deepen your understanding of transmutation, consider studying the principles of alchemy. Alchemy is not merely a historical practice of turning base metals into gold; it is a metaphor for personal transformation. The alchemical process involves the dissolution of the old self to create a new, more refined version. This concept can be applied to your own life as you work to transmute negative energy patterns into positive ones.

Incorporate rituals into your practice to honor the process of transmutation. Create a sacred space where you can engage in these rituals, lighting candles or burning incense to enhance the atmosphere. Consider performing a ritual bath infused with herbs or essential oils known for their purifying properties. As you soak, visualize the negative energy being released from your body and replaced with light and love.

You may also wish to create a crystal grid to support your transmutation efforts. Crystals such as amethyst, black tourmaline, and clear quartz are known for their protective and healing properties. Arrange these crystals in a geometric pattern that resonates with your intention for transformation. As you meditate near your crystal grid, visualize the energy of the crystals amplifying your intention and facilitating the release of negativity.

As you progress on your journey of transmuting negative energy patterns, it is essential to maintain a positive mindset. Affirmations can serve as powerful tools for reinforcing your intention and shifting your perspective. Create affirmations that resonate with your goals for transformation, such as, "I release all negativity and embrace the light within me," or "I am a vessel of love and harmony." Repeat these affirmations daily, allowing their energy to permeate your consciousness.

Engaging with nature can also enhance your transmutation practice. Spend time outdoors, connecting with the natural world and allowing its energy to rejuvenate you. Nature has an innate ability to cleanse and purify, helping you release negative energy patterns. Take a walk in the woods, sit by a river, or simply bask in the sunlight. As you immerse yourself in nature, visualize the earth's energy flowing through you, washing away any negativity and replacing it with peace and tranquility.

As you navigate the intricate process of transmuting negative energy patterns, remember that you are not alone. Seek support from like-minded individuals or communities that resonate with your journey. Sharing your experiences and insights with others can provide valuable perspectives and encouragement as you work through the challenges of transformation.

21

Working with Elemental Energies

"The elements are the building blocks of life; they are the forces that shape our existence and guide our spiritual journey."

Invariably, the mastery of elemental energies demands that you engage deeply with the primordial forces of earth, air, fire, and water, each embodying unique vibrational signatures that can be harnessed for profound spiritual transformation. To attune yourself to these elemental frequencies, you must first acknowledge their intrinsic qualities. Earth signifies stability and grounding; air epitomizes intellect and communication; fire embodies transformation and willpower; and water reflects emotion and intuition.

Begin your journey by immersing yourself in the essence of Earth. Visualize roots extending from your body into the soil, anchoring you to the planet's core. Feel the weight and solidity of the earth beneath you, allowing its stabilizing energy to permeate your being.

This process not only grounds you but also fortifies your connection to the material world. As you connect with the earth, you may wish to incorporate physical practices such as walking barefoot on grass or soil, engaging in gardening, or simply spending time in nature. These activities deepen your relationship with the earth element, enhancing your sense of stability and security.

Next, engage with the element of air. Imagine yourself as light as a feather, floating in a gentle breeze. Take a few deep breaths, letting the air fill your lungs and expand your chest. This practice increases your potential for mental clarity and acuity, allowing you to tap into the intellectual and communicative qualities of air. As you exhale, visualize releasing any mental clutter, making space for higher wisdom and telepathic insight. You can enhance this experience by practicing breathwork techniques, such as pranayama, which can help you cultivate a deeper connection to the air element and its associated energies.

Once you have established a connection with earth and air, it is time to invoke the transformative power of fire. Visualize a vibrant flame at your solar plexus, radiating warmth and illumination. This inner fire serves as a catalyst for your willpower, empowering you to manifest your intentions and dissolve energetic blockages. Focus on this flame, allowing its energy to ignite your passions and drive. You may choose to incorporate rituals involving fire, such as lighting candles or creating a small bonfire, to symbolize the transformative power of this element. As you engage with fire, remember to respect its power and use it responsibly, recognizing it as both a source of energy and a force of destruction.

After connecting with fire, turn your attention to the element of water. Visualize a serene body of water, perhaps a calm lake or a gentle stream. As you immerse yourself in this imagery, allow the qualities of water to wash over you. Water embodies emotion, intuition, and fluidity, reminding you of the importance of adaptability in your life. Take a moment to reflect on your feelings and emotions, allowing the energy of water to cleanse and purify any negativity or emotional blockages. You can enhance this experience by spending time near a body of water, such as a river, lake, or ocean, or by incorporating water rituals into your practice, such as taking a cleansing bath or creating a water altar.

As you work with these elemental energies, it is essential to recognize the interconnectedness of the elements. Each element influences and interacts with the others, creating a dynamic balance that shapes your spiritual journey. For example, the stability of earth supports the fluidity of water, while the transformative power of fire ignites the intellect of air. By understanding these relationships, you can cultivate a more harmonious existence, integrating the energies of each element into your daily life.

To deepen your connection with elemental energies, consider creating an elemental altar in your sacred space. This altar can serve as a focal point for your practice, allowing you to honor and work with the energies of earth, air, fire, and water. You might include representations of each element, such as crystals, herbs, candles, or images that resonate with you. As you engage with your altar, take time to meditate on each element, inviting its energy into your being and allowing it to guide your spiritual growth.

In addition to creating an altar, you can explore the use of elemental correspondences in your rituals and spellwork. Each element is associated with specific herbs, crystals, colors, and symbols that can enhance your connection to its energy. For example, earth is often linked to grounding stones like hematite or black tourmaline, while air is associated with clear quartz or amethyst. Fire corresponds with red or orange candles, while water is connected to blue or green hues. By incorporating these correspondences into your practice, you can amplify the energies you are working with and create a more potent spiritual experience.

As you continue to explore the elemental energies, consider the importance of balance in your life. Each element possesses both positive and shadow attributes, and it is essential to recognize and integrate both aspects. For instance, while fire can represent passion and transformation, it can also manifest as anger or aggression if not properly channeled. Similarly, water can embody healing and intuition, but it can also lead to emotional overwhelm if not balanced. By cultivating awareness of these dynamics, you can create a more harmonious relationship with the elements and ensure that they support your spiritual journey rather than hinder it.

Engaging with elemental energies can also provide valuable insights into your personal growth and development. Each element has unique lessons to teach, and by working with them, you can gain a deeper understanding of yourself and your place in the universe. For example, earth teaches the importance of grounding and stability, while air encourages intellectual exploration and communication. Fire ignites your passions and willpower, while water invites you to embrace your emotions and intuition. By reflecting on the qualities of each element, you can identify areas of your life where you may need to focus your attention or cultivate greater balance.

As you work with elemental energies, consider incorporating movement practices such as yoga or dance into your routine. These practices can help you connect with the physical aspects of each element, allowing you to embody their energies in a more tangible way. For example, grounding poses in yoga can help you connect with the earth element, while flowing movements can enhance your connection to water. Fire can be expressed through dynamic, powerful movements, while breath-focused practices can deepen your relationship with air. By integrating movement into your practice, you can create a holistic approach to working with elemental energies.

In moments of difficulty or challenge, remember that the elemental energies are always available to support you. When you feel overwhelmed, turn to the grounding qualities of earth to stabilize your energy. If you need clarity, breathe deeply and connect with the expansive qualities of air. When facing obstacles, invoke the transformative power of fire to ignite your willpower and drive. And when emotions arise, allow the healing energy of water to cleanse and purify your spirit. By consciously engaging with these elements, you can navigate life's challenges with greater ease and grace.

22

Developing a Personal Energy Practice

"The universe is made of energy, not matter."

Setting out on the journey to develop a personal energy practice requires a deliberate alignment of your inner will with the universal currents that shape our reality. This alignment isn't merely a conceptual understanding; it is an experiential immersion into the subtleties of the energetic tapestry that interweaves all existence. To embark on this path, you must first contemplate the resonant frequencies that vibrate within your being, tuning into the harmonic symphony that echoes through your mind, body, and spirit.

Begin by establishing a sanctified space—an energetic nexus where your practice can flourish. This space should be free from external disruptions and imbued with symbols that resonate with your higher self. You might choose to employ sacred geometry, talismans, or crystals to amplify the vibrational field around you. Each of these elements serves as a conduit for higher energies, enhancing your connection to the universal life force.

As you enter this sacred space, invoke a state of meditative stillness that allows your consciousness to transcend mundane distractions. Breathing techniques are paramount in this practice. Inhale deeply, drawing prana, the life force, into every cell of your being. As you exhale, release not just air but any discordant energies that may obstruct your inner vision. Visualize a radiant light enveloping your form, harmonizing with the cosmic frequencies that permeate the universe.

Next, cultivate a daily practice of energy manipulation exercises. Techniques such as Qi Gong, Reiki, or Kundalini Yoga can serve as conduits for mastering the flow of energy. These practices not only enhance your ability to sense and direct energy but also deepen your understanding of the intricate dynamics of your energy body. As you practice, focus on your chakras, imagining them as vortices of swirling energy, each attuned to specific vibrational frequencies. Using the power of intention, direct energy to align these centers, ensuring an unobstructed flow.

As you engage in these practices, you will develop an acute sensitivity to the subtle energies that govern existence. This sensitivity enables you to mentally control the energy field with precision and intent. The mastery of energetic projection is not an end in itself; rather, it is a gateway to deeper esoteric knowledge and understanding.

To further enhance your personal energy practice, consider incorporating additional techniques that promote energetic alignment and growth. One such technique is the practice of mindfulness. Mindfulness encourages you to remain present and aware of your thoughts, emotions, and sensations. By cultivating this awareness, you can better recognize the subtle shifts in your energy and respond accordingly. Mindfulness can be practiced during meditation or integrated into your daily life, allowing you to maintain a heightened state of awareness throughout your day.

Another powerful method for developing personal energy is through the practice of gratitude. Gratitude is a high-vibrational state that can significantly enhance your energetic field. By regularly expressing gratitude for the blessings in your life, you create a positive energetic resonance that attracts more abundance and positivity. Consider keeping a gratitude journal, where you write down the things you are thankful for each day. This practice not only reinforces your positive mindset but also amplifies your personal energy.

Engaging in creative expression is another effective way to develop your personal energy. Activities such as painting, writing, dancing, or playing music allow you to channel your energy into tangible forms. Creative expression serves as a release valve for emotional energy, enabling you to process and transform your feelings into something beautiful and meaningful. This process not only enhances your personal energy but also fosters a deeper connection to your true self.

As you continue to refine your personal energy practice, it is essential to maintain a strong connection to your physical body. The body serves as the vessel for your energy, and nurturing it is crucial for energetic development. Prioritize self-care practices, such as regular exercise, a balanced diet, and sufficient rest. These foundational elements support your overall well-being and create a solid foundation for your energetic work.

In addition to physical self-care, consider incorporating practices that promote emotional and mental well-being. Techniques such as journaling, therapy, or engaging in supportive relationships can help you process and release any emotional blockages that may hinder your energetic flow. By addressing these underlying issues, you create space for new, positive energy to enter your life.

As you deepen your personal energy practice, you may encounter challenges or obstacles along the way. It is essential to approach these experiences with curiosity and openness. If you find that your energy feels stagnant or blocked, take time to reflect on any underlying emotions or beliefs that may be hindering your ability to project effectively. Engaging in practices that promote emotional release, such as journaling or energy healing, can help you clear these blockages and restore the flow of energy.

Another important aspect of developing personal energy is the cultivation of a supportive community. Surrounding yourself with like-minded individuals who share your interests and goals can provide valuable insights and encouragement. Consider joining a group focused on energy work, meditation, or personal development. The collective energy of a supportive community can amplify your practice and foster a sense of belonging.

As you progress on your journey of developing personal energy, remember that this process is not a race. Each individual's journey is unique, and it is essential to honor your own pace. Celebrate your progress, no matter how small, and trust that each step you take brings you closer to your goals.

To further enhance your personal energy practice, consider exploring various modalities of energy work. Techniques such as acupuncture, massage therapy, or sound healing can provide additional support for your energetic development. These practices can help release tension, promote relaxation, and facilitate the flow of energy throughout your body.

23

Integrating 33rd Degree Knowledge into Daily Life

"The universe is not outside of you. Look inside yourself; everything that you want, you already are."

As you begin to integrate 33rd Degree knowledge into your daily life, you will embark on a transformative journey that elevates your conscious awareness and aligns your actions with the universal currents that shape our reality. This integration is not just an intellectual exercise; it is a profound practice that requires you to embody the principles of higher wisdom in every aspect of your existence. By fostering a mindful awareness that transcends mundane perception, you can elevate your daily actions into sacred expressions of this knowledge.

The first step in this integration process is to establish a daily energy ritual. These rituals serve as a foundation for your practice, allowing

INTEGRATING 33RD DEGREE KNOWLEDGE INTO DAILY LIFE

you to cultivate a deeper connection with your inner self and the universe. Begin each day with an invocation to align your inner vibrational frequency with the universal harmonics. This could involve a simple morning meditation or a more elaborate ritual that resonates with your personal beliefs and values.

Visualize prismatic light channels emanating from your core, merging with the celestial ether. This practice anchors your consciousness to the ethereal domains, forging a conduit for divine energy to permeate your aura. As you engage in this visualization, allow yourself to feel the warmth and vibrancy of this light, knowing that it is a reflection of your true essence.

Breathwork is another essential component of integrating 33rd Degree knowledge into your daily life. Engaging in rhythmic breathwork synchronizes your inhalations and exhalations with the oscillations of the Earth's geomagnetic fields. This attunement amplifies your psychospiritual resonance, allowing you to harness the latent energies within and around you. As you breathe deeply, envision each inhalation drawing in cosmic energy, while each exhalation releases any residual stagnation.

Contemplate the sacred geometry present in natural forms, recognizing the fractal symmetries that manifest the cosmic blueprint. Sacred geometry is a powerful tool for understanding the interconnectedness of all things and can serve as a guide for your daily practices. By incorporating symbols such as the Flower of Life or the Golden Ratio into your rituals, you align yourself with the fundamental patterns of the universe, enhancing your energetic flow.

Incorporating ritualistic movements into your daily practice can also be transformative. Techniques such as Qi Gong or Kundalini Yoga embody the flow of cosmic currents and serve to ground and elevate your energetic vibration. These movements, performed with intentionality, act as a catalyst for transmuting lower vibrational frequencies into higher states of consciousness. As you engage in these practices, focus on the sensations within your body, allowing the energy to flow freely and harmoniously.

As you develop your personal energy practice, it is essential to remain aware of the subtle energies that influence your daily life. Pay attention to the people, environments, and situations that resonate with your energy and those that do not. This awareness allows you to make conscious choices about where to direct your energy and how to protect yourself from negative influences.

Creating a sacred space in your home can also support the integration of 33rd Degree knowledge into your daily life. This space should be a reflection of your personal journey and a sanctuary for your spiritual practices. Decorate this space with items that resonate with your higher self, such as crystals, candles, and sacred symbols. Regularly spend time in this space, engaging in meditation, reflection, or any practices that nurture your spirit.

In addition to establishing a sacred space, consider incorporating daily affirmations into your routine. Affirmations are powerful tools for reshaping your beliefs and aligning your thoughts with your intentions. Choose affirmations that resonate with the principles of 33rd Degree knowledge, such as "I am connected to the universal energy that flows through all things" or "I embody the wisdom of the cosmos." Repeat these affirmations daily, allowing their vibrations to permeate your consciousness and reinforce your commitment to your spiritual growth.

INTEGRATING 33RD DEGREE KNOWLEDGE INTO DAILY LIFE

Engaging with nature is another essential aspect of integrating 33rd Degree knowledge into your daily life. Nature serves as a powerful reminder of the interconnectedness of all living beings and the energetic currents that flow through the universe. Spend time outdoors, whether through hiking, gardening, or simply sitting in a park. As you connect with the natural world, take note of the energies present in your surroundings. Observe the patterns, colors, and movements of plants and animals, allowing them to inspire your own energetic practice.

As you cultivate this connection with nature, consider incorporating elements of the natural world into your rituals. This could involve using natural materials, such as flowers, stones, or water, in your practices. Each element carries its own unique energy and can enhance your connection to the earth and the cosmos.

Another powerful way to integrate 33rd Degree knowledge into your daily life is through acts of service and compassion. By extending your energy to support others, you create a ripple effect that amplifies the positive vibrations in the world. This could involve volunteering, offering emotional support to a friend, or simply practicing kindness in your daily interactions. Each act of service is a reflection of the higher wisdom you embody, reinforcing your connection to the universal energy that flows through all beings.

As you continue to integrate these practices into your daily life, it is essential to remain open to the lessons and insights that arise along the way. The journey of spiritual growth is not always linear; it often involves periods of introspection, challenge, and transformation. Embrace these experiences as opportunities for growth and understanding, knowing that each step you take brings you closer to embodying the principles of 33rd Degree knowledge.

Regularly reflect on your progress and the ways in which you have integrated this knowledge into your life. Consider keeping a journal to document your experiences, insights, and intentions. This practice not only provides a space for self-reflection but also serves as a powerful reminder of your commitment to your spiritual journey.

As you deepen your understanding of 33rd Degree knowledge, you may wish to explore additional resources that can support your growth. Books, workshops, and online courses can provide valuable insights and techniques for further integrating this wisdom into your daily life. Seek out communities or groups that resonate with your interests, allowing you to connect with others who share your journey.

Incorporating mindfulness into your daily routine is another effective way to integrate 33rd Degree knowledge. Mindfulness encourages you to remain present and aware of your thoughts, emotions, and surroundings. By practicing mindfulness, you cultivate a deeper connection to your energy and the energies of those around you. This heightened awareness allows you to respond to situations with intention and clarity, aligning your actions with your higher self.

Consider setting aside time each day for mindfulness practices, whether through meditation, mindful eating, or simply taking a few moments to pause and breathe. As you cultivate this awareness, you will find that your ability to integrate 33rd Degree knowledge into your daily life becomes more fluid and intuitive.

As you master the art of integrating this knowledge, you will likely notice shifts in your energy and experiences. You may find that you attract opportunities, resources, and people who align with your goals and aspirations. This phenomenon is often referred to as the Law of Attraction, which suggests that like attracts like. By raising your vibrational frequency through focused intention and mindful practice, you create an energetic alignment that draws your desires closer to you.

24

A Symphony of Enlightenment

"The only journey is the one within."

Having laid a strong foundation through daily energy practices, the next evolutionary phase involves nurturing mindful energy awareness, thereby seamlessly intertwining the intricate threads of 33rd Degree knowledge into the fabric of your everyday life. This elevated state of consciousness engages you in a harmonious dance with the energy frequencies that pervade the cosmos. You become the adept navigator, finely attuned to the subtle vibrations that ripple through the etheric realm.

To embark on this sacred journey, start by consciously tuning your inner senses to the oscillations of your surroundings. Visualize the energy currents as radiant threads, each pulsating with an ancient resonance. Through this heightened awareness, you can discern the symbiotic relationships between your internal energy matrix and the external energy fields. Utilize the Hermetic principle of mental transmutation to elevate your vibrational frequency. This alchemical process involves transforming lower vibrational states into higher ones through concentrated intent and focused thought. As you refine this skill, you'll notice a synchronization between your mental state and the universal energy flow, leading to synchronicities and enhanced intuition.

Incorporate mindful energy awareness into everyday tasks, transforming them into sacred rituals. This integration bridges the esoteric and the ordinary, allowing the profound wisdom of the 33rd Degree to illuminate your path. In the ongoing process of elevating conscious thought, you will weave the profound threads of 33rd Degree knowledge into the very essence of your daily existence, turning mundane moments into conduits of spiritual enlightenment.

As an adept, you must rise above the ordinary by tuning your mind to the subtle symphony of universal frequencies. Each thought, infused with the sacred geometry of higher wisdom, becomes a catalyst for transformative change, converting the heavy pull of daily distractions into the golden essence of awakened awareness. By consciously aligning your mental vibrations with the harmonic resonance of the cosmos, you will activate your inner sanctum—the source of divine insight.

Engage in contemplative practices that elevate your cognitive frequencies, such as meditative visualization and affirmations, to foster a heightened state of conscious perception. Through this disciplined integration, your awareness expands, enabling you to perceive the intricate interconnections that underlie reality. To achieve a harmonious balance of energy flows and seamlessly weave 33rd Degree knowledge into your daily life, cultivate a conscious awareness of the subtle energetic currents that permeate your being and environment.

Interact with the vibrational frequencies by tuning your inner resonance to the cosmic symphony surrounding you. Begin each day with meditative practices that anchor your spiritual essence, strengthening your energetic core and aligning it with universal rhythms. Visualize the flow of pranic energy coursing through your chakras, each vortex spinning in harmonious convergence. Feel the pulsations of the Earth's magnetic field and allow them to guide your grounding processes.

Engage in energy-balancing techniques such as Tai Chi or Qigong, which harmonize the microcosmic orbit of your intrinsic energy with the macrocosmic order. Maintain a continuous connection to the etheric plane by practicing mindful breathing, allowing your breath to weave a luminous tapestry that interlaces through your auric field. Use mantras and sacred geometries to recalibrate any dissonant frequencies, fostering a state of serene balance.

By embracing these esoteric methodologies, you transcend ordinary existence and embody the transcendent wisdom of the 33rd Degree, ensuring a balanced and enlightened flow of energy in every aspect of your life. Amidst the complexities of your daily existence, intertwine the sacred principles of the 33rd Degree by infusing each moment with intentionality and spiritual awareness, transforming mundane tasks into rituals of profound significance.

When you awaken, visualize your energy field aligning with higher frequencies—a symphony of vibrations harmonizing with the cosmos. As you nourish your body, contemplate the sacred geometry of your sustenance, recognizing each bite as a conduit of universal energy. Throughout your day, practice mindfulness not merely as a mental

A SYMPHONY OF ENLIGHTENMENT

exercise but as a mystical act of attunement. Each breath becomes a sacred invocation, each step a pilgrimage toward enlightenment.

By weaving 33rd Degree knowledge into your routines, you establish a sanctified rhythm—a cadence resonant with the divine. Engage in reflective meditation, acknowledging the cyclical nature of time and the eternal now. Connect with the energy frequencies permeating your environment, mentally attuning to their subtle currents. When you retire for the night, visualize an aura of protection and healing enveloping you—a cocoon of recharged energy.

This harmonization of daily routines with 33rd Degree principles transforms ordinary existence into a continuum of spiritual evolution. You have now embarked on a journey akin to tuning a cosmic orchestra. Picture an ancient alchemist transforming lead into gold; you are transmuting raw energy into enlightened awareness. Remember, one small shift in your energy field can ripple through the universe. As you master these frequencies, you are not just altering your reality; you are harmonizing with the divine symphony. Trust in your intuitive compass and let the ancient secrets of the 33rd Degree illuminate your path.

Printed in Great Britain
by Amazon